The Tragi-Comic Professional

The Tragi-Comic Professional

Basic Considerations for Ethical Reflective-Generative Practice

by
Paul Dokecki

DUQUESNE UNIVERSITY PRESS
Pittsburgh, Pennsylvania 15282

Published in the United States of America by
DUQUESNE UNIVERSITY PRESS
600 Forbes Avenue
Pittsburgh, PA 15282-0101

Library of Congress Cataloging-in-Publication Data

Dokecki, Paul R.
The tragi-comic professional: basic considerations for ethical reflective-generative practice / by Paul R. Dokecki.
p. cm.
Includes bibliographical references and index.
ISBN 0-8207-0269-2. — ISBN 0-8207-0270-6 (pbk.)
1. Human services personnel — Professional ethics.
2. Psychotherapists — Professional ethics. 3. Professional ethics.
I. Title.
HV10.5.D65 1996
174'.936 — dc20

96-9981
CIP

Contents

Preface

I address this book to a variety of professionals. Although I am a psychologist, with interests in community, clinical, and developmental psychology, I want to speak beyond my discipline in attempting to convince members of the helping or caring professions, broadly understood, that *the essential purpose of professional practice is to promote the common good through the enhancement of the client's human development and of community.* This purpose, moreover, is an expression of the human condition that is tragi-comic: as human beings, necessarily imperfect, we can never fully succeed in achieving our purposes — the human tragedy. But we can and should try to be ethical and can succeed to a meaningful extent in influencing the realms of human development and community — the human comedy.

My intention is to develop a rationale for this tragicomic human development and community viewpoint under the heading of *reflective-generative practice.* The phrase *basic considerations* in the book's subtitle suggests my orientation. In teaching ethics to graduate and undergraduate students with a variety of emerging professional interests, I have found few books specifically related to professional ethics that go beyond "how to" or casebook orientations to the development of fundamental understandings of the place of values and ethics in the professional's life world. Professionals typically view ethics as a separable aspect of practice they invoke only when they encounter an "ethics alert." I argue that professionals must understand their calling, both in their interventions and in their systematic inquiry, as ethical to the core, and they should understand the ethical obligations they incur in this calling in the context of the tragicomic human condition.

I develop this thesis through philosophical argument — mainly based in social phenomenology (Berger and Luckmann, Buber, Farley, Mayeroff, Levinas, Ricoeur), the philosophy of action (Bernstein, Macmurray, Toulmin), and, incongruously to some readers because it departs from these traditions, virtue ethics (Aristotle, Aquinas, and, especially, MacIntyre). I complement this philosophical mode of analysis with highly selected professional examples — mainly in the areas of psychotherapy and interventions for families and children — not to test a fully developed model, which my position is *not,* but to help develop and specify the model further. I do not pretend to offer a method or algorithm for deciding among ethical alternatives, nor do I present case material to illustrate specific courses of ethical action. Rather, I ask readers to consider the most fundamental aspects of their practice and to "try on for size" and critically evaluate a reflective-generative orientation and its first principles of community and human development. I invite readers into a basic conversation about the nature of ethics and the professions.

My approach to professional ethics is postpositivist, transactional, and ecological. It derives largely from the insights I gained from almost twenty years as a faculty member in Peabody College's Transactional-Ecological Psychology (TEP) Program. Operating in the spirit of Nicholas Hobbs's view of psychology in the public interest, colleagues (J. R. Newbrough, Jeanne Plas, and Jules Seeman) and I provided training in community, clinical, counseling, and school psychology that was value-based and ethically-grounded, appreciative of human diversity, and pertinent to human development problems of concern to the public interest. I owe a debt I can never repay to the colleagues and students who made TEP a community of scholars in the most meaningful sense of that overworked phrase. In the years since TEP ended, several of my students have continued to keep aspects of that community alive for me, especially Harriet Able-Boone, Stacy Coleman, Craig Anne Heflinger, Luann Klindworth, and Michele Sokoly. Several other colleagues have also significantly influenced my thinking, especially Rev. James K. Mallett, Robert Moroney of Arizona State University, and Robert O'Gorman of Loyola University Chicago. O'Gorman, Newbrough, and I formed the Reflective Practice Group, an interdisciplinary research and consultation team focusing on community and organizational development.

To paraphrase the Beatles and Joe Cocker, I get by intellectually with a little help from my friends. Since the mid 1980s, I have been strongly influenced by my friend and colleague Richard Zaner, Ann Gedes Stahlman Professor of Medical Ethics and director of Vanderbilt's Center for Clinical and Research Ethics, in which I am a member, through his phenomenological clinical liaison ethics (see chapter 2). And as I began this book, I sought help from my friend and colleague Edward Farley, Drucilla Moore Buffington Professor of Theology at the Vanderbilt Divinity School. After reading his important book *Good & Evil* (Farley, 1990), I realized that his phenomenological analysis might function as one of the conceptual foundations of my version of professional ethics. During an extended conversation, I sketched my emerging position and how I would use and extend his ideas. Shared understanding was immediate. I thank him for his inspiration and continued support, but the responsibility for the use of his ideas is, of course, mine alone.

I had known of Ed Farley's distinguished body of work for many years. Then, in 1990, the event happened that eventually immersed me in his *Good & Evil.* We had originally met in the late 1970s at a jazz jam session. He now invited me to join a jazz group he was forming — Farley plays jazz trumpet, and I have been an aspiring jazz drummer since my high school days in Brooklyn during the 1950s. The new group began playing as *Good & Evil* appeared. During some of our musical conversations, we acknowledged that we probably had shared intellectual interests beyond jazz. I finally read his book because, based on our jazz interactions, I had an intuition, now abundantly rewarded, that it would be relevant to my work. The fruits of Farley's influence are apparent throughout this book, and I explore his position in detail in chapter 2.

For years, I have been intending to write about jazz as a metaphor for ethics and social intervention in pursuit of the common good and now take initial steps to do so. The jazz experience and metaphor have influenced me at one level or another throughout my academic life. It has helped me envision an approach to professional ethics intended mutually to enhance (a) personal freedom and creativity — in short, the *human development* of clients and professionals — and (b) cooperative action in *community*. This two-sided agenda forms the ethical core of what I have come to call reflective-generative practice.

The Introduction and chapter 1 set the societal context for the development of the ethics of reflective-generative practice and introduce the jazz metaphor and the notion of professional action as a practice. In chapter 2, I lay the conceptual groundwork for the ethics of reflective-generative practice, mainly through several dimensions of social phenomenological analysis. Chapter 3 continues the development of this ethical framework, including coverage of some of the more typical topics in professional ethics (character, prima facie and actual duty, the virtues, power, communication, and the like), viewed in the context of reflective-generative practice. This chapter uses the currently acute ethical problem of professionals having sex with their clients. It also delves into considerations of the nature of the professional-client transaction to elaborate the tragicomic, mixed-motive nature of professional life, wherein professional power may be used for both human development and self-aggrandizing, manipulative purposes. Finally, chapter 4 develops the broader community and public policy ethical implications of reflective-generative professional life.

Introduction

The Professional as Jazz Musician

In the varied topography of professional practice, there is a high, hard ground overlooking a swamp. On the high ground, manageable problems lend themselves to solution through the application of research-based theory and technique. In the swampy lowland, messy, confusing problems defy technical solution. The irony of this situation is that the problems of the high ground tend to be relatively unimportant to individuals or society at large, however great their technical interest may be, while in the swamp lie the problems of greatest human concern. — Donald A. Schön, *Educating the Reflective Practitioner*

Music and tragic myth are to an equal extent expressions of the Dionysiac capacity of a people, and they are inseparable. Both originate in a sphere of art beyond the Apolline. Both transfigure a region in whose chords of delight dissonance as well as the terrible image of the world charmingly fade away; they both play with the sting of displeasure, trusting to their extremely powerful magical arts; both use this play to justify the existence even of the 'worst world'. Here the Dionysiac, as against the Apolline, proves to be the eternal and original artistic force, calling the whole phenomenal world into existence; in the midst of it a new transfiguring illusion is required if the animated world of individuation is to be kept alive. If we could imagine dissonance becoming man — and what else is man? — then in order to stay alive that dissonance would need a wonderful illusion, covering its own being with a veil of beauty. That is the real artistic intention of Apollo, in whose name we bring together all those innumerable illusions of the beauty of appearance, which at each moment make life

worth living and urge us to experience the next moment.
— Friedrich Nietzsche, *The Birth of Tragedy*

It don't mean a thing if it ain't got that swing. — Duke Ellington

The professions are in crisis. The crisis is one of legitimacy and of confidence, self and public, shared by the professions with most of society's major institutions — government, the military, religion, education, corporate business, and the like. The professional crisis has its own dynamics, however, with prominent ethical and methodological features. Ethically, professionals have lost touch with the major reason for their practice, their ethical center, namely, as I shall argue, *to foster the human development of their clients and thereby to promote the common good.* Methodologically, their approaches to generating usable knowledge have typically been limited and inadequate to their practical tasks and the confusing problems they face. (I explore methodological issues in every chapter.)

In this last decade of the twentieth century, we are busily fulfilling many of the prophecies Erich Fromm (1955) made in *The Sane Society,* a deeply ironic title for a book analyzing the *insane* society we have been creating in the modern world. We have been behaving like machines, like robots, dehumanizing each other in our selfish, narcissistic, egotistical, over competitive, not sufficiently cooperative, and characteristically masculine (macho) pursuit of power. We are a society that not only tolerates but also invites the abuse of power.

Professionals are among those who, on behalf of their

clients and the good of society, should be leading the effort against the abuse of power. But, as we shall see, they sometimes fall prey to the temptation to use the power inherent in their professional roles primarily for their own good and only incidentally or accidentally for the good of others, as their codes of ethics and professional traditions demand. A dramatic and disturbing instance of such professional abuse of power is that of professionals having sex with their clients. This behavior, the subject of endless movies and television scripts, is increasing in public awareness and all too common among a wide variety of professionals, including physicians, psychotherapists, teachers, ministers, lawyers, and the like. As I suggest in chapter 3, professional-client sex is an instructive microcosm of the larger set of ethical issues besetting contemporary professional life.

As a long time listener and aspiring player of jazz, I have gradually come to view it as having metaphorical meaning much beyond the immediacy of the pleasure and challenge it provides to the audience and the musician. But what could jazz possibly have to do with ethics and the professions?

The utility of my mostly intuitive and unexpressed use of the jazz metaphor became apparent in an extended encounter in the summer of 1991 with Martin Williams, the late jazz critic, musicologist, and historian. Williams came to Vanderbilt from the Smithsonian to offer a course on jazz history. He put jazz in philosophical and societal context, insightfully expressed in two passages from his classic, *The Jazz Tradition* (Williams, 1959/1993):

> First, jazz knows of no absolutes: there is no one "best" way of performing a piece. Each day, each moment has its

> way, and hence its own meaning. Tomorrow's way is not today's; today's is not yesterday's.
>
> That does not mean that there are no standards. Yesterday's way may have been better than today's, or not as good. Tomorrow's may be better still or less good. And I may be perfectly clear and specific about where the inferiority or superiority lies. But I accept such differences as inevitable and natural, and I take each day's way of performing for its own meaning. At the same time, my standards themselves change with my own growth and change. And I accept these changes too.
>
> Thus, in several respects, the dimension of time is acknowledged in the nature of the music. And, again, there are no absolutes.
>
> Philosophically, then, jazz is a twentieth-century music. Through *doing*, jazz musicians have arrived at, and have lived, a fundamental insight of contemporary philosophy. (p. 262)

Thus, Williams relates jazz to the philosophy of action and to the enduring issue of relativism versus absolutism, very much in the spirit of Bernstein's (1983) *Beyond Objectivism and Relativism* and the argument I advance in chapter 2. He argues for standards, but he rejects both relativism (the view that any idea is as good, bad, or indifferent as any other) and absolutism (the view that there is one and only one acceptable body of ideas). He acknowledges the influence of historical context, suggesting the power of tradition, and maintains that standards can and do apply in making judgments of goodness. These musical judgments may be aesthetic ones, but Williams is making a general point about judgment, including ethical judgment.

Williams then addresses the traditional tension between the individual and the social encountered in ethics and social-political philosophy:

> No music depends so much on the individual as jazz. Indeed, jazz requires not only an individual interpretation of melody, it demands spontaneous individual invention of new melody, individual articulation of emotion, and individual interpretation of musical sound.
>
> No jazz player is supposed to sound like any other player. A musician's instrumental voice should be as uniquely personal as is his speaking voice, but obviously its quality must be more a matter of deliberate, conscious development than that of his speaking voice. One could probably tell the history of jazz in terms of the way in which this concept of individual sound has been developed, modified, and enlarged over the years.
>
> But at the same time that jazz depends on the individual, it also depends on group co-operation. In all its styles, jazz involves some degree of collective ensemble improvisation, and in this it differs from Western music even at those times in its history when improvisation was required. The high degree of individuality, together with the mutual respect and co-operation required in a jazz ensemble carry with them philosophical implications that are so exciting and far-reaching that one almost hesitates to contemplate them. It is as if jazz were saying to us that not only is far greater individuality possible to man than he has so far allowed himself, but that such individuality, far from being a threat to a co-operative social structure, can actually enhance society. (p. 263)

Williams identifies, therefore, the potential for *mutual enhancement of the person and the community.* The individual person and the social realm can and should be seen as necessary for each other's survival, development, and ethical mode of being.

To illustrate the power of the jazz metaphor, I draw on my musical acquaintance, referred to in the Preface, with Edward Farley, the author of *Good & Evil.* The first time we and several other jazz musicians played together several years ago, we engaged in *group cooperation* and *collective ensemble improvisation,* to use Williams's terms. Our particular group of musicians had never played together before. Several persons met for the first time in the rehearsal hall. We decided to start with Dizzy Gillespie's composition, "A Night in Tunisia." As leader, Farley established the tempo, and we were off and playing. Verdict? Not bad for a first tune ever for this group: We started together, played in support of each other throughout, and several solos were original, even impressive. After finishing (together!) with the standard, but complicated, ending, there was a collective "yeah!" of satisfaction. And all this happened in the immediacy of the moment, with no prior rehearsal. The group permitted and encouraged individual creativity as it came together as a manifestation of artistic process.

Many jazz uninitiates, including my three rock music loving daughters, think that jazz is often formless and incomprehensible. Where is the melody? Musicians play anything they wish as the mood strikes them. There is no rhyme or reason. It is freeform anarchy. The reason that our new jazz group could play together from the outset, however, is that jazz is highly structured. Most jazz standards, like "A Night in Tunisia," are played according to a more or less set pattern established by the jazz tradition, a tradition created by the countless times members of the jazz community have played a particular tune over the years throughout the country and the world. Experienced jazz musicians know many tunes — their musical form, usual tempo, rhythm, melody, and harmonic structure. These make up the rules of the music, and a musician's *duty* is to absorb this tradition and have the skill to execute it on the spot. This is what has made possible many of the "blowing sessions" captured on records over the last seventy five years that have contributed so much to building the jazz tradition. "Paying one's dues," required for entry into the world of jazz players, means making the tradition thoroughly and competently one's own. The jazz tradition provides the standard by which players are judged. It suggests to them how to "do the right thing" — in moviemaker Spike Lee's terms (the first of many allusions to movies throughout this book).

As Williams points out, however, the tradition's strictures and structures provide the context for "spontaneous individual invention." The major figures in the history of jazz have been the soloists and innovators — Louis Armstrong, Duke Ellington, Coleman Hawkins, Lester Young, Billie Holiday, Charlie Christian, Dizzy Gillespie, Charlie Parker, Theolonious Monk, Miles Davis, Sonny Rollins, John Coltrane, Ornette Coleman, to name a few. In Williams's words, which bear restating: "Individuality, far from being a threat to a co-operative social structure, can actually enhance society." Thus, it is possible to view *personal* development and *social* development as mutually enhancing, not necessarily antagonistic, as Freud and much of the Western intellectual tradition have viewed them to be. But jazz shows us a picture more complicated than that, entailing the two familiar levels of the personal and the social, but highlighting an often overlooked third level, that of the intersubjective or interhuman.

The practice of jazz makes demands on the musician as *person* continually to develop and extend musical technique, and to visit and revisit the jazz tradition. It is a hard task master, constantly requiring the jazz player to do the right thing. But when a musician merely plays technically in rule-bound fashion, the result is not jazz, since, as Duke Ellington said, making music, however competently, "don't mean a thing if it ain't got that swing." Improvisation, creativity, and human development are at the heart of jazz. Thus jazz yields a glimpse of the demands of the personal side of human existence, wherein each individual person is called to develop humanly, fully to actualize her or his potential.

Jazz, however, is also a *social* practice (chapter 2). It has its history and tradition, its economics and politics, its heroes and villains. The aspirations of the emerging jazz musician include coming under the influence of and mastering the tradition, finding an individual creative voice, and at the highest level, making a contribution so creative that the tradition itself changes to reflect it.

The "top down" of jazz as social practice merges, therefore, with the "bottom up" of the jazz player as person, and the music, at its best, mutually expresses the grandeur of the social and the creativity of the person. This schematic requires for completion consideration of the immediate medium for this merger of perspectives. This is the intersubjective, face-to-face encounter (chapter 2), in what might be called the interhuman realm, of the members of a jazz group (the solo jazz performer is a special case not considered here) as they make the music.

Louis Armstrong's Hot Fives and Sevens, the Count Basie and Duke Ellington orchestras, Art Blakey's Jazz Messengers (sometimes called "the university of Art Blakey" because of its enormous influence over the years on its individual members and on the jazz tradition), the Max Roach-Clifford Brown Quintet, several of Miles Davis's groups, John Coltrane's classic quartet, to name but a few are truly great jazz groups. In the act of playing, they manifested among their members very high levels of communication, mutual listening and respect, empathy of telepathic proportions, and other signs of intense interpersonal relationship. Jazz players and listeners, alike, readily recount those truly thrilling instances when a group jells in coming together to make moving and innovative music. The musicians "do the right thing," and the result is a swinging and creative integration of the personal, the interhuman, and the social realms of human existence. Such *peak moments* do not always happen — jazz musicians, after all, are imperfect tragicomic human beings subject to personal and social distractions like the rest of us — but they set the standard for excellent practice, and lure players and listeners into devotion to the music.

A variety of musicians from diverse national and ethnic backgrounds have competently and creatively engaged in the social practice of jazz during the twentieth century. My listings above of great, innovative players and groups are anything but complete. Virtually no critic or scholar, however, would question any of those listed, and many would be reluctant to add others if innovation that contributed to the jazz tradition was the sole criterion for inclusion. It may be surprising to some and awkward to others to discover that *all* those I have listed are products of African-American culture.

Although scholars have offered many reasons, some of which are highly controversial, for the disproportion of African-Americans in the jazz pantheon, I believe Martin Williams had *the* fundamental insight. Related at least in part to the history of oppression experienced by African-

Americans in the United States, the genius of jazz, argues Williams, lies in its deep appreciation of human suffering and *tragedy*, nonetheless expressed positively, even *comedically*— but realistically and without undue optimism. In effect, jazz is a tragicomic social practice expressing the faith and hope of a community that believes it shall overcome. This community, moreover, invites all of us, as players or listeners, into the midst of their practice.

What is the nature of the phenomenon referred to by this term *practice*, and what are its implications for professional ethics? Answers to these questions are fundamental to the ethical framework I develop in this book.

1
The Professional Dual Relationship: Goods Internal and Goods External to a Practice

Professionals claim to contribute to social well-being, put their clients' needs ahead of their own, and hold themselves accountable to standards of competence and morality. But both popular and scholarly critics accuse the professions of serving themselves at the expense of their clients, ignoring their obligations to public service, and failing to police themselves effectively. — Donald A. Schön, *The Reflective Practitioner*

Tragedy perishes when deprived of the spirit of music just as sure as it can be born only in that spirit. . . . We must stride boldly into the thick of those battles which, as I have said, are being waged in the highest spheres of the contemporary word between insatiable optimistic knowledge and the tragic need for art. — Friedrich Nietzsche, *The Birth of Tragedy*

One of the basic considerations I offer for discussion in this book is that a *tragicomic dual relationship* is at the heart of professional practice. This relationship entails a tension between the pursuit of goods internal to a professional practice (human development and community) and goods external to it (other goods, such as money and self-gratification, selfishly pursued by the professional, often through the manipulative or exploitive use of professional power). *Tragic* refers here to the inevitable imperfection of human actors that interferes with attainment of the goods they seek; *comic* to the goods humans can achieve, within limits, if they intend them and exert themselves to achieve them.

A serious professional ethical problem exemplifying the tragicomic is the unfortunately rampant phenomenon of professionals from many disciplines having sexual relations with their clients. This problem entails practitioners pursuing their own agenda (goods external to their practice), usually as a matter of the use and abuse of power, at the expense of human development and community (goods internal to their practice). Although professionals are inevitably tempted, and although many succumb, they are ethically called not to abuse their power in this way. All can, and most do, summon the strength and courage not to do so. I return to this particular phenomenon in chapter 3; here I elaborate the general nature of a dual relationship through explicating the nature of a practice.

The Professions as Practices

A *practitioner*, according to the computerized *American Heritage Dictionary*, is, obviously enough, "one who practices something, especially an occupation, a profession, or a technique." The associated noun is *practice,* one definition being the "exercise of an occupation or a profession," as in the practice of law, medicine, social work, teaching, or psychotherapy. A practitioner is a professional person who engages in a practice to do good, in the context of our present discussion, to promote human development and community.

More generally, says Alasdair MacIntyre (1981), a practice is "any coherent and complex form of socially established human activity through which goods internal to that form of activity are realized in the course of trying to achieve those standards of excellence which are appropriate to, and partially definitive of, that form of activity, with the result that human powers to achieve excellence, and human conceptions of the ends and goods involved, are systematically extended" (p. 175). On this view, tic-tac-toe, kicking a football, bricklaying, planting an apple tree, operating an electron microscope, playing a musical scale, and interpreting a dream are not practices, while chess, the game of football, architecture, farming, biology, jazz, and psychotherapy are. "Thus the range of practices is wide: arts, sciences, games," and more broadly, "politics in the Aristotelian sense, the making and sustaining of family [and community] life, all fall under the concept" (p. 175).

A professional practice, then, entails a complex set of actions and dispositions (knowledge, skills, competencies, and values) that are coherently organized. It is socially established, having its origin in the life of the community. Moreover, it is structured and can be evaluated according to generally and traditionally accepted standards of excellent practice, which themselves emanate from and are constitutive of the practice. Thus, over time, practitioners evolve and extend the nature of their professional endeavors, retaining the best of the past and looking to new developments in the future. At any given time, professional community members can and do make judgments of what constitutes good and bad, competent and incompetent, ethical and unethical practice. Such judgments are far from relative and arbitrary, as suggested by Williams's analysis of jazz in the Introduction, emanating as they do from the history and tradition of the practice and embodied in those who have achieved the status of recognized authorities or masters in a field. These authorities are among the persons who socialize new members into the practice through teaching, serving as role models and mentors, and arbitrating current practice.

A practice is defined or has meaning as a practice in terms of the ends or goods it is socially established to achieve and its codified and systematic means for achieving these goods. We may call these goods, after MacIntyre, *goods internal to a practice.* The achievement of internal goods, says MacIntyre, contributes, in win-win fashion, to the overall good of the community. All community members are better off for their attainment. The excellence and ethics of a practice are judged relative to the goods practitioners achieve and how they achieve them, *within the context of the practice community itself.* In the realm of sports, for example, relative to the history and traditions of basketball, both in the way he plays the game and in his remarkable achievements in the game per se, Michael Jordan deserves the accolade *excellent performer.* The same could be said of an excellent jazz musician such as Wynton Marsalis, chess player such as Bobby Fischer, lawyer such as Thurgood Marshall, surgeon such as Michael DeBaky, or psychotherapist such as Jules Seeman. The enormous sums of money Michael Jordan receives for engaging in the practice of basketball undoubtedly constitute goods, however, they are *not* goods *internal* to the practice.

The phenomenon of money being paid to practitioners introduces MacIntyre's companion concept, *goods external to a practice.* These goods, says MacIntyre, are characteristically competed for, and there are winners and losers. Competition for external goods and many other factors beyond a practice inevitably penetrate and influence the pursuit of goods internal to it, creating a tragicomic situation. Practices never exist in isolation but in complex social contexts and are inevitably mixed-motive affairs. So Michael Jordan may say that he wants to play basketball solely for the love of the game, but would he be playing as well and as long as he is without the incentive of goods external to the practice of basketball, including the adulation of the fans and the enormous sums of money he is paid? In his tumultuous career, was the influence of these external goods getting out of hand, distracting him, beginning to get in the way of his excellent practice,beginning to bring into stark relief the tragicomic nature of his situation? Here we begin to glimpse that some form of blending of internal and external concerns or of resolving the tension between them is necessary to achieve the kind of excellent and ethical professional practice that promotes human development and community.

The all too common manifestation of the tragicomical in jazz — where, for example, legendary musician Lester Young scuffled throughout his musical career and died penniless — in no way diminishes the excellence of his body of work. Bertrand Tavernier's masterful film, *Round*

Midnight, portrays the last days of a struggling African-American jazz musician — a composite of two jazz greats, Bud Powell and Lester Young, both of whom set standards for goods internal to the practice of jazz yet always seemed to lack external goods. On the other hand, there are many musicians who have betrayed their art and debased the goods internal to the practice of jazz for the sake of achieving fame and making large amounts of money.

Goods internal to a professional practice are pursued primarily in the intersubjective face-to-face transaction between client and professional that transpires in the interhuman sphere of human existence. Pursuit of such goods entails professional *persons* treating clients as *persons* and caring for them in pursuit of mutual human development and community. Consistent with the Introduction's analysis of jazz, factors that compete with the single-minded pursuit of these internal goods, giving rise to a tragicomic condition, occur both in the spheres of the individual practitioner as personal agent and the social-institutional world that contains or surrounds the practice. What does this mean?

The Sphere of the Individual Practitioner as Personal Agent

The client and professional transact in the professional situation in order to enhance the client's (and thereby the professional's) human development and community, which are the goods internal to professional practice. Each is a personal agent with a particular tragicomic life story or narrative comprising: (a) *past* experiences (and attendant psychodynamics) concerning significant events and persons (parents, siblings, friends, peers, teachers); (b) *present* actions, motivations, priorities, and projects; and (c) *future* intentions, goals, and purposes. Life narratives can be understood through a combination of methods (Polkinghorne, 1988), including a kind of psychoanalytic archeological exploration of the past, phenomenological analysis of present experience, and teleological probing of transcendent future life directions. When such a narrative is mature and well developed and serves the person well, it has meaning and may be termed a *generative narrative.* Another way of understanding the goods internal to professional practice, then, is in relation to the client's generative narrative: the professional's task is to help the client enhance (or create) and enact a generative narrative, in the context of tragicomic life experiences. This analysis also suggests that society expects the professional person to have a mature and well-developed, albeit tragicomic, generative narrative. More on narrative later.

Competent and effective professional actions relative to the client's generative narrative constitute the hallmark or regulative ideal of excellent and ethical reflective-generative practice. Among the factors threatening the pursuit of the goods internal to a practice are the evil and tragic dimensions of the personal sphere (to be investigated in chapter 2 with the help of Farley's social phenomenology). These personal-level threats to generativity may be understood, at least in part, in terms of psychodynamics. Simply put, having faulty or immature personality development may lead professionals to be tempted to emphasize their own rather than the client's agenda, to pursue goods external to their practice, rather than to enhance the client's human development and community. For example, therapists who have had sex with their clients tend to exhibit personally and socially problematic behavior often involving power and control, anger, and sadism (Sonne and Pope, 1993). Selfishness, egotism, or narcissism may, therefore, come unduly to influence the client-professional transaction and cause external goods to be given priority over internal ones. Professionals may freely intend to put their needs ahead of their clients' needs and thereby exploit them, use them as means to their own ends, or they may inadvertently do so because of psychopathological factors — what used to be loosely called neurosis. In either case, society expects professionals to be mature enough, even though their life world is tragicomic, to be ethical and not to succumb to these self-centered concerns. Professionals should both (a) have been carefully chosen for entry into their profession on the basis of their virtue or strength of character, making it highly likely that they can be trusted to strive in the highest ethical fashion to work unselfishly on behalf of their clients and to give higher priority to goods internal than to goods external to their practice, and (b) have been helped to become aware of their faults and immaturities and take steps to correct them during the process of professional socialization. Problems on either of these two counts raise serious ethical concerns.

As hard as individuals and professional socialization agents who have the responsibility of developing or improving their personal qualities as emerging professionals may try, however, every professional person inevitably practices with mixed motives entailing goods both internal and external to their professional practice. For example, all therapists are probably sexually attracted to at least some of their clients some of the time. Such attraction, however, is in no way unethical. Acting on the attraction is unethical, however, because there is a strong presumption that such action entails the abuse of professional power, as we shall see in chapter 3.

Ethical professional practice in the context of the mixed motives of tragicomic human existence is highly demanding. In Sisyphean fashion, it often feels like rolling a very large rock up a very steep hill. As suggested above, such practice requires the practitioner to have a mature generative narrative, to have strength of character — in a word, to be *virtuous* in the tragicomic life world. To speak of virtue in professional ethics is to emphasize the enduring habits or characteristics developed over time that come to distinguish the overall nature of a professional person's life. "We have to accept as necessary components of any practice with internal goods and standards of excellence the virtues of justice, courage, and honesty" (MacIntyre, 1981, p. 178). Taken together with the virtues of trustworthiness, prudence, and caring (elaborated in chapter 3), these virtues are among those that define practitioners' relationships with clients and with each other. *Justice* entails fairness — treating like persons alike and different persons differently on the basis of their needs; *courage* enables the professional to meet ethical practice's taxing demand to do the right thing; and *honesty* is the very foundation of a practice, since a practice couldn't exist if practitioners weren't honest with themselves and their professional colleagues, as well as with their clients (Bok, 1978).

The Sphere of the Social-Institutional World

Pursuit of the client's human development and community as goods internal to professional practice is also compromised, made tragicomic, by the fact that practices never occur in a vacuum. They are embedded in social context, in a web of service delivery, governmental, and professional institutions and organizations with their priorities, agendas, and values. This social-institutional world inevitably creates tensions as it pushes for the achievement of goods external to practices, often entailing economic matters. For example, therapists or physicians may be tempted to use their professional power to extend treatment with certain clients even though they may not need it, because the clinic or hospital needs the money, and there may be insurance or other form of third-party payer to provide it. After all, the rent and light bill must be paid, and the children must be sent to college. This fairly obvious example illustrates a ubiquitous tragicomic issue in professional life: Practices of every sort — from medicine and psychology to education and ministry to law and engineering — must be economically sound in order to survive, to exist to pursue their internal goods.

In the era prior to the 1960s, George Kelly — the eminent personality theorist, psychotherapist, university professor, and, incidentally, my internship psychotherapy supervisor — is said to have refused to take money for therapy because it interfered with the therapeutic task. Although his position challenges us ethically, perhaps he could afford to take it because he operated within the shelter of an academically sponsored clinic. Then and now, of course, such economic shelter is rare, even in academia.

An ongoing tragicomic ethical tension facing professionals, then, is to secure the external economic goods required to sustain their practice while being steadfast in pursuing the internal human development and community goods that are the reason for and sine qua non of the practice in the first place. In these days of pressures to reduce the national debt, to reform the health care and welfare systems, to practice defensively to forestall malpractice threats, and to be accountable to clients, resolving this tension in favor of achieving the goods internal to a practice — the professional ethical imperative — is becoming increasingly difficult and is growing in importance as a challenge to ethical professional life.

In a different but related vein, the social-institutional world usually values certain styles of practice, typically those characterized by technical rationality. Technical rationality (explored further in chapter 3) may not always be conducive to meeting clients' needs, may not help them create or enhance their generative narrative. In other words, the social-institutional world may make it difficult for professionals to engage ethically with their clients. Social-institutional changes are required.

In regard to these needed changes, an important influence of the social-institutional world in creating tensions between goods internal and external to professional practice is in the realm of ideology and societal values. The phenomenon of client-therapist sexual relations provides a useful clue to some of the key ideological influences. The demographics of that phenomenon — the offending professional almost always is male — suggest the undeniable operation of gender-related ideological factors. As in society at large, men, in this instance therapists, often abuse their power to take advantage of women, in this instance clients. I argue that one of the foundational barriers to ethical professional practice, a tragicomic cultural manifestation, is that of the still pervasive and powerful traditional constructions of gender. In so arguing, however, I do not wish to exacerbate the seemingly inevitable and sometimes destructive tension between traditionally masculine and feminine values. Rather, I intend to help ameliorate this tension and help move society toward a more constructive value position, one that is more conducive to ethical professional practice than the prevailing masculine value position that strongly influences the professional world. (See chapter 3 for an elaboration of the gender issue).

In conclusion, professionals doing the right thing in the client-professional transaction, namely, giving priority to goods internal rather than external to their practice — within the tragicomic matrix of human existence as personal, interhuman, and social — is the core of the position I develop and argue for in this book. In the professional-client transaction, the parties should be understood as personal agents who bring their life stories with them onto the interhuman stage of professional practice. The professional's ethical task is two-sided — (1) to subordinate egoistic concerns in favor of enhancing the client's human development and (2) to contribute to the development of community — while operating in an institutional context that may call for pursuit of competing agendas.

Keeping the jazz metaphor in mind, with its mutual concern for the personal and the social, will help in navigating some of the abstract and complex matters that must be pursued in developing an ethical reflective-generative framework for professional practice. The next chapter contains a reconceptualization of professional action, termed reflective-generative practice, to establish that ethics is central to and constitutive of the professional enterprise.

2

Initial Steps Toward an Ethical Model for Reflective-Generative Practice

The face in its nakedness as a face presents to me the destitution of the poor one and the stranger. . . . The poor one, the stranger, presents himself as an equal. . . . He comes to *join* me. But he joins me to himself for service. . . . The *thou* is posited in front of a *we.* To be *we* is not to "jostle" one another or get together around a common task. The presence of the face, the infinity of the other, is a destituteness, a presence of the third party (that is, of the whole of humanity which looks at us), and a command that commands commanding.
— Emmanuel Levinas, *Totality and Infinity*

Like institutions, agents constitute a distinctive sphere of human reality which human evil works to isolate from the face. The very existence of a community of

> the face is a displacement of that isolated sphere. The reality of this community is not the mediation of resources to separate agents but of agents-in-relation under the face and before the sacred. — Edward Farley, *Good & Evil*

> There is no knowledge that is not power. — Ralph Waldo Emerson

To understand professional ethics as the response to ethical storms that periodically arise on the otherwise calm, value-neutral, and technological sea of professional practice seriously misconceives the nature of the professions. The too typical image of a professional who only thinks of the ethical dimensions of practice when a crisis arises should trouble us. Should I report my client to the police since he threatened to kill his wife this evening? Reach for the professional code of ethics. Am I bound to hold confidential my client's admission that she violently abuses her young son? What does the ethics code say? Well into a professional relationship, I find that my client can't afford to pay. What does the code say I should do? How far should I go in acting out the sexual attraction I have toward my client? Where is that code anyway?

Not that ethical critical incidents are unimportant. When professionals narrow their moral-ethical understanding to these isolated instances, however, they miss dimensions of the client-professional transaction that are central and pervasive, not peripheral and episodic. I argue that professional practice is value-laden, ethical to the core, tragicomically awash in a sea of power issues manifested in the tension between the developmental use and manipulative abuse of power. It entails a continual process of discerning, deciding, and acting ethically. Intervention has ethical dynamics pertaining to the client and professional as persons, the relation between them, and the social institutional context of this relation of persons. In medical ethics, my colleague Richard Zaner's (1988, pp. 243–46) clinical-liaison ethics[1] addresses the complexity of this process.

---

[1] Zaner's intellectual tradition is phenomenology. His practice of clinical-liaison ethics as applied phenomenology is in the spirit of the social ecological tradition established in the early 1960s by Peabody College's Nicholas Hobbs in Project Re-ED, a nationally implemented intervention program for emotionally disturbed children (Hobbs, 1966, 1982). Hobbs was my mentor, friend, and colleague (Hobbs et al., 1984), and I later worked closely with Zaner (Dokecki and Zaner, 1986) and continue to do so. Some of the work my colleague J. R. Newbrough and I did with Zaner in the mid 1980s led him to incorporate liaison thinking into clinical ethics.

The liaison function is a central aspect of the Re-ED philosophy. It is grounded in a transactional and ecological understanding of deviant behavior. On this view, the key to understanding human development and its problems does not reside exclusively in either the person or the environment but in their transaction — in the fit or lack of fit between a person's capacities and the environment's demands. The liaison specialist in Project Re-ED actualizes this understanding: "The function of the liaison person is to help members of an ecosystem conceptualize what keeps the system from working, identifying sources of discord, modify behaviors, mobilize resources required to achieve shared goals, and acquire the capacity to deal with excessive discord in the future" (Hobbs, 1982, p. 215).

There are many similarities between Re-ED's liaison function

On Zaner's view of the professional encounter: (1) Ethics should focus on how the client(s) and the professional(s) as involved persons define the situation. (2) Moral issues arise within the concrete situation as experienced by the involved persons. (3) The persons in the situation are the principal resources for resolving the moral issues. Moreover, (4) this encounter exists in historical and institutional context, with many traditional roles and duties, that exerts powerful but often unexamined influence on the transactions between clients and professionals. The client-profession encounter, in other words, is a complex system. I argue that such complexity requires inquiry grounded in transactionalism to fully comprehend it.

A Transactional-Ecological Perspective

Transactionalism holds that primitive understandings of human phenomena exclusively focusing on *either* person *or* environment (self-actionalism) must be replaced by more developed views recognizing the joint action of *both* person *and* environment (inter-actionalism or transactionalism) (Dewey and Bentley, 1949). The most developed view, transactionalism, is analogous to the Einsteinian concept of space-time in which space and time are no longer understood as separate dimensions but

---

and Zaner's clinical-liaison ethics. The difference is that Hobbs addresses the *professional* working with troubled and troubling clients, while Zaner addresses the *applied ethicist* working with professionals working with clients. Hobbs's liaison function has ethical implications; Zaner's clinical liaison ethics has intervention implications. Both are transactional and ecological in outlook and are in the spirit of reflective-generative practice.

as integrally related in one space-time continuum. The transactional view of human development is *ecological,* identifying the person-environment unit as fundamental for knowing human development. One of the forebears of the ecological tradition in psychology, Kurt Lewin, observed more than fifty years ago that behavior is a function of the person and the environment, or in the shorthand of his famous equation, B = f (P, E). This suggests the critical importance of studying person-environment transactions. My intent in this chapter is to develop a transactional-ecological ethical framework — in the spirit of Zaner's clinical liaison ethics and of Lewin's life and work — as a foundation for reflective-generative practice.

The transactional-ecological perspective suggests that we socially construct and negotiate reality. Reality is "neither 'in the head' or 'out there' in some positivistic aboriginal form" (Bruner, 1990, pp. 105–6). The postpositivist human sciences, in whose spirit I write, reject all methodological claims to be the royal road to knowledge (Bernstein, 1983). This is so since the quest for the Archimedean point of absolutely certain objective knowledge, by positivism or by its methodological competitors, is misguided and has not been achieved. If we cannot achieve absolutely certain objective knowledge in our tragicomic state, however, this doesn't mean we can't achieve any usable knowledge. We can usefully view knowledge as assertoric.

The notion of *assertoric knowledge* suggests that "some knowledge claims are better than others, but none is beyond doubt" (Polkinghorne, 1983, p. 289). Moreover, the logic of assertoric knowledge differs from deductive logic. Assertoric knowledge entails argumentation and practical reasoning. We decide among alternatives, each of which falls short of certainty. An assertoric inquirer argues before a community of inquirers by providing evidence and attempting to show that his or her assertion is the most plausible among rival alternatives. Assertoric knowledge, therefore, is neither absolute and objective nor relativistic. Argumentation within a community in pursuit of its values and practical objectives establishes the truth and validity of knowledge (Bernstein, 1983; Dokecki, 1987, 1990, 1992). Recall Williams's analysis of jazz in the Introduction.

Ethics and Relativism: The Argument against Emotivism

The view of knowledge as assertoric requires that we address the charge that ethical inquiry is so relative as to be meaningless — devoid of cognitive content or truth value. The metaphor for this problem is the Tower of Babel, a "symbol of our moral condition" (Stout, 1988, p. 1). Modernity, argues Stout, has eroded "our confidence in the idea that truths or justified beliefs *can* be attained by ethics" (p. 3). Moreover, this erosion of confidence can have troubling and potentially destructive effects on how we live our everyday and professional lives in the community.

We must attempt to become clear about how we come to know social reality and the nature of our knowledge once attained. There are, according to Berger and Luckmann's (1966) social phenomenology, three cyclical moments in developing our knowledge: the person *externalizes* (constructs) the meaning of social reality that has been experienced; the person *objectifies* this externalized construction; the person *internalizes* the once externalized and now objectified construction in the ongoing process of socialization. Some persons over attend to the objectifying moment of this process and are naively realistic with a fundamentalist view of the social order and role expectations. They reify (from the Latin *res, rei*— thing; therefore, reify = "thingify") what has been socially constructed. Others overemphasize the externalizing moment and are subjectively idealistic, relativistic, and even solipsistic about the social world with its roles and ethically relevant role expectations. They fall prey to the intellectually and ethically corrosive relativistic view that any social construction is as good, bad, or indifferent as any other. Thinking, reasoning, and ethics thereby become highly problematic, and we are left being ethically relativistic, skeptical, even nihilistic.

Full appreciation of the three moments of this process of social construction yields a sophisticated view of reality as simultaneously there, to be known with confidence, and continually interpreted and reinterpreted in the knowing-known transaction. We are, argue Berger and Luckmann, born into an already existing social world that is for us simultaneously humanly constructed, objectively experienced, and socially produced. Our world, says Kelly (1955, p. 6) "is a real world, not a world composed solely of the flitting shadows of people's thoughts. But . . . people's thoughts also really exist, though the correspondence between what people really think exists and what really does exist is a continually changing one." We construct social reality, and can and must reconstruct it, in order to make our way in the social world. But relativism, especially in the guise of *emotivism*, poses significant challenges to our living in this socially constructed world and engaging in meaningful ethical inquiry.

Inquiry involving rational argument and evidence *can* enrich ethical discourse and help improve the quality of intervention decisions (see Dokecki et al. [1986] for a review of the positions and arguments). This assertion challenges the prevailing beliefs of our emotivist culture. Emotivism is "the doctrine that all evaluative judgments and more specifically all moral judgments are *nothing but* expressions of attitude or feeling [and] . . . are neither true nor false" (MacIntyre, 1981, pp. 11–12). Emotivism entails the view that inquiry is incapable of securing agreement about moral or value judgments, because they are merely and only subjective and relativistic preferences.

Inquiry's enmeshment with values and ethics has emerged as a theme in many critiques of mainstream social science's limitations and failures. These critiques identify ways in which inquiry *might* and *should* address values and ethics. The argument is that inquiry in general, and ethical inquiry, in particular, are value-laden but capable of valid and generalizable knowledge. There are, however, too few instances of inquiry that *does* in fact address ethical matters through rational inquiry and ethical discourse. The legacy of emotivism stands in the way of this latter form of inquiry.

The tension between the currently dominant position of emotivism, a highly individualistic and relativistic position, and more community-based alternative positions, such as the reflective-generative position I am developing here, has deep roots in human personality and culture. The issue is not just epistemological; there are equally important existential dimensions. Agency (the individualistic principle) and communion (the community principle) have operated in tension throughout human history. Each person and each society arrives at its own tragicomic agency-communion blend or balance. The triumph of agency over communion has increasingly come to characterize the modern world, and emotivism is one of the fruits. One of the major tasks of our age is to mitigate agency with communion (Bakan, 1966). This is so because the societal gains from the ascendancy of individualistic agency and emotivism have reached a point of diminishing returns, and the human requirement for community has been increasingly unmet in the modern era, to the detriment of human development and the common good.

On the emotivist view, facts and values are always separate, and moral and ethical views possess only the authority claimed for them by the individual. In opposition to this view, says MacIntyre (1981, p. 264), "to understand our central evaluative and moral concepts is to recognize that there are certain criteria we cannot but acknowledge. The authority of those standards is one that we have to recognize, but of which we are in no way the originators." This alternative to individualistic emotivism insists on the importance of a *moral community* embodying moral and evaluative concepts that have meaning beyond the autonomous individual person, as with assertoric knowledge and the jazz metaphor.

Paternalism, Autonomy, or Community?

These initial considerations of emotivism highlight its epistemological and methodological implications and its emphasis on the autonomous individual as the sole authority for ethical judgments. The matter goes beyond epistemology, however, to everyday life where ethics tragicomically plays out in action.

The image of the autonomous individual is a vivid one in contemporary society, especially in current biomedical ethics. In the early 1970s, for example, patients were attempting to free themselves from the "tyranny of technology" (Veatch, 1984, p. 38). This struggle was embodied in the challenge posed by the principle of autonomy to the traditional principle of Hippocratic paternalism, which had physicians do whatever they believed to be in the best interests of the patient. Great benefits ensue, argues Callahan (1984), when autonomy is given moral priority, including (a) a respect for individual rights and personal dignity, (b) protection against political and moral oppression, (c) a healthy tentativeness about moral claims, and (d) the provision of a rationale for protecting the minority from the majority. For these and other reasons, argues Veatch (1984, p. 38), "the case is overwhelming that autonomy takes moral precedence over paternalism," but this is "a temporary triumph of autonomy" (p. 40), since autonomy is a principle with implications limited to the special situation where its competitor is the principle of paternalism.

Although useful and necessary, autonomy manifests the tragicomic and often has socially corrosive uses in everyday life. These community-threatening aspects of autonomy include (a) the prevailing beliefs that each person is a moral agent sealed off from others, (b) all social relationships are contractual and voluntary, (c) respect for my autonomy is all that others owe me and I them, and (d) morality is at base relativistic and subjective (Callahan, 1984).

Since the principle of individual autonomy produces many benefits, meddling with it is perilous. But, argues Callahan (p. 40), "autonomy should be a moral good, not a moral obsession. It is a value, not the value." Autonomy tends to erode many essential features of ethics, including "piety toward tested and long-standing moral traditions, a search for morality in the company of others, community as an ideal and interdependence as perceived reality, and an embracing of autonomy as a necessary but not a sufficient condition for a moral life" (p. 40). We must mitigate the principle of autonomy with a concern for community, recognizing that the tragicomic individual is a member of a moral community. Again recall the jazz metaphor with its mutual concern for the person and the community.

Within a moral community (exemplified historically in the *polis* of Aristotle's Athens), MacIntyre (1966) argued:

> when I say, "You ought to do this," or when I say, "This is good," I want to protest that I say more and other than, "You or anyone else — do this!". . . . For if that is what I mean, that is what I could and would say. If that is what I do say, then certainly what I say will have no authority but that which I confer upon it by uttering it. My attitudes and my imperatives have authority for me just because they are mine. But when I invoke words such as ought and good I at least seek to appeal to a standard which has other and more authority. If I use these words to you, I seek to appeal to you in the name of those standards and not my own name. . . . You cannot use the moral vocabulary and consistently deny the force of ought, and you cannot remain within the social commerce of the community and abandon the moral vocabulary. (pp. 264–5)

This passage suggests a clash between two views of ethics. First, there is the modern majority view of individualistic and relativistic emotivism — exemplified, says MacIntyre, by Nietzsche's[2] position that an individual's will to power is the basis for morality, that the person who carries the biggest stick wins the day for his or her subjective moral position. Second, there is the decidedly minority view of ethics within a coherent moral community, exemplified by Aristotle's position that a moral community can use reason, based on external ethical standards, to establish a moral position (MacIntyre, 1981).

The reflective-generative practitioner holds for the reason-based Aristotelian position over the power-based Nietzschean position. The reason for this choice is that human development and community grow in the soil of social practices informed by reason and conversation; they wither and die in the context of fear, coercion, and violence. The Aristotelian position I endorse is consistent with the view of knowledge as assertoric, a matter of Aristotelian practical reasoning (*phronesis*) enacted in the community's social practices.

Reflective-generative practice entails a position counter to emotivism, the pervasive and often hidden agenda of modern relativistic ethical thinking. We now should turn to a more detailed development of reflective-generative social practice.

---

[2] The quotes from Nietzsche I used to open chapters 1 and 2 were from his earliest work, *The Birth of Tragedy*, which he later repudiated, but which contains certain enduring observations, especially about tragedy and music.

The Essence of Reflective-Generative Practice[3]

The role of *reflective practitioner* derives from Schön's (1983) exhortation to professionals to be reflective in response to the crisis of the professions that characterizes our age. Reflective practice requires changes in both the professional's and the client's role expectations. It calls for the client and the professional to enter a partnership of shared responsibility involving joint exploration of their situation — reflection-in-action. The professional's tragicomic relationship with the client is, in effect, one of reflective conversation, which requires "double vision": the reflective practitioner as inquirer, according to Schön, must "(1) impose an order of his own on the situation [vision #1], (2) take responsibility for the order he imposes, (3) hold himself open, at the same time he imposes order, to the situation's 'back talk' [vision #2]" (p. 163).

Many professionals assume the responsibility of inquiring through *basic* research and theorizing relevant to the world of practice. Yet other professionals engage in systematic research and development to improve practice broadly. Still others systematically inquire to help plan, implement, and evaluate policies that influence human development and the practice of human development professionals. The professional is ethically obligated both to inquire and to be ethical in this continuum of inquiry.

The reflective practitioner, then, is an intervention agent and inquirer who intends to enhance human development

---

[3] This section appeared in somewhat altered form in Dokecki (1992).

and thereby the common good through the close interplay of knowledge use and knowledge generation. The reflective practitioner, however, intends to avoid the dualism of practice and theory. Recall Kurt Lewin's famous dictum that nothing is so practical as a good theory (Marrow, 1969). Theory here is reflection inspired by the challenges of practice. Rather than operating within positivism-empiricism's methodology of technical rationality, which insists that practice is legitimate when and only when it derives from scientifically tested theoretical knowledge, the reflective practitioner sees inquiry as transactionally arising from the very practice of intervention. Knowledge is practical; practice yields knowledge. The logic is one of practice-theory-practice (Browning, 1991).

A role that complements that of the reflective practitioner is the *generative theorist* (Gergen, 1978). This is an intervention agent and inquirer who pursues the development of theory to improve the human situation according to rationally chosen values. The generative theorist intends to avoid the dualism of fact and value (Fischer, 1980) and seeks to enable persons-in-community to develop and become contributors to the common good and the public interest.

Erik Erikson's (1967) concept of generativity is also relevant here. Generativity is a developmental achievement, the culmination of the human developmental process (Browning, 1973). Browning (p. 151) characterizes Erikson's theory as "descriptive and normative ecology," in pursuit of making persons strong. Strong, for Erikson, means capable of meeting life's tasks and thereby developing humanly. If the reader has been asking just what I mean by human development, my answer is that I mean by it what Erikson means by it — growth over the life span culminating in generativity. Reflective-generative practice, therefore, intends to enhance Eriksonian human development, a position we may call the "Ethics of Human Ecology" (Browning, p. 151). But what are the roots of this position? First, here are some very basic and essential considerations.

Transcendence: The Nature of the Person and the Source of Ethics

Interventions by reflective-generative practitioners and the ethics that guide them concern, in the context of the tragicomic human situation, an *is-ought discrepancy.* We evaluate a situation as it is (interpreted through the lenses of our values); the situation ethically challenges us because we find it lacking compared with our values, our standards of what ought to be; and we intervene to lessen or remove the situation's is-ought discrepancy. In effect, as tragicomic agents, we attempt to discern and enact an effective and ethical intervention strategy — in Spike Lee's terms, to *Do the Right Thing.* Selected film allusions help advance our thinking.

It is not easy either to know or to do the right thing. *Do the Right Thing* portrays incendiary racial tensions in Brooklyn with deep historical roots, exacerbated by late twentieth century forces that aggravate animosities and make choice of right action difficult to discern. Even if we should succeed in discerning an ethical course of action — the film presents the choice between the ways of Martin Luther King and Malcom X — Lee suggests that the pressures of current society make enactment of this choice extraordinarily difficult. Thus, Lee's film is a cautionary tale for ethics, professional and otherwise: Ethical discernment and enactment are hard tasks to master, are, as I have been suggesting, played out in the context of the tragicomic life world.

What is it about our society that makes knowing what is right to do and then doing it so difficult? John Sayles's ironic title for his film *City of Hope* suggests one answer. In effect, Sayles portrays a city of *No* hope, a tragic place where immediate selfish and narcissistic concerns preoccupy us and lock us into an extremely harsh social reality. Virtually every character in the film — especially the males — attempts to use whatever power or advantage he can claw out of his daunting social reality to manipulate, coerce, and exploit others. Other human beings are things — alienated, depersonalized, dehumanized — used for his own ends. All that matters is his own agenda, what he wants in the present situation. Sayles portrays an intricate web of social relations dominated by a double helix of motives: (1) fear-driven protecting of self from threat and (2) fear-driven threatening of others for personal gain.

Hope, on the other hand, manifests a comic outlook. It implies a realm or epoch beyond us, a better time and place than our present situation, anticipated with longing and expectation. It implies transcendence of the immediate here and now. There is, however, virtually no hope in the *City of Hope*, and it is every man (sic) for himself in an immediacy ruled by the Machiavellian use of power to manipulate and coerce. To live in the world Sayles depicts is to encounter on a day by day basis an (un)ethical position so pervasive that other possible ethical positions are virtually buried. If by some miracle we discern one, it meets opposition on all sides by the prevailing social and institutional structure. Such a world would be described by Erich Fromm (1955) as *insane*, and a chilling recurring symbol in the film is a homeless psychotic man who mindlessly repeats to those around him the crazy things he hears in his daily life in Sayles's virtually hopeless world. Sayles shows us a tragicomic vision, emphasizing, however, the tragic — what we should ethically struggle against and why such a struggle is so exacting. There may be hope, but it is only there nascently and requires much effort to develop.

John Sayles made *City of Hope* as a radically negative object lesson, a deeply ironic portrayal of the ethical dimensions of life. Lawrence Kasdan is his film-making alter ego. His film *Grand Canyon* portrays a vision of contemporary life fully appreciative of the tragic, evil, and unethical tendencies Sayles depicts. Kasdan, however, explicitly states the comic ethical position Sayles ironically implies, in effect emphasizing the comic in the tragicomic.

In an early and crucial scene, Kasdan depicts an affluent white man who gets lost at night in a poor section of Los Angeles after a Laker game. African-American gang members terrorize him when his expensive car breaks down. He rightly fears for his property and his life, and we empathize with him. A tow truck arrives, driven by a middle-aged African-American man who also recognizes the life-threatening danger in the situation. He could easily drive on, avoid what he knows would also be a threat to his life, and leave his customer-to-be to fend for himself. We would understand and empathize with this action as well. But he doesn't leave. He intervenes, believing it is his duty, and after much intimidating language and gesturing by the youths, he convinces them to leave without violence, allowing them to save face.

We learn that this tow truck driver believes there are realms of existence that transcend his own immediate situation, symbolized by the Grand Canyon. When he visited there prior to the film's action, he was overwhelmed, realizing that his everyday tragic life circumstances and problems paled in comparison to the canyon's vastness and mystery. This experience, somehow connected to his other encounters with the transcendent, reinforced his predilection to care for others, suggested by his longstanding caring relationship with his daughter who has a hearing impairment. He becomes the center of a web of personal relationships among the film's characters — black and white, men and women, young and old — who conquer their fears and enact the human tragicomedy by reaching beyond themselves to care for others. He makes Los Angeles a city of hope for those whom he touches, and the film ends with their visiting the Grand Canyon as one grand extended family.

The Grand Canyon as a force in the lives of Kasdan's characters symbolizes the transcendent — a realm beyond the self, beyond the immediate, the sensible, the measurable. Transcendence heightens appreciation of tragic human fragility and imperfection, and we see each other, in comic fashion, as persons worthy of love, respect, and care, clinging to each other in community to make our way in a difficult and threatening world. Transcendence, I will argue, is fundamental and foundational for ethics. This argument begins with Freud.

In *Freud and Philosophy,* Paul Ricoeur (1970), noted phenomenologist, engaged in a critique of Freud's archeological theory of sublimation. Freud's theory is archeological in the sense of his going back in time and excavating layer after layer of psychic material to get to the psychological heart of current thoughts, feelings, and actions. Ricoeur's analysis raises the question of whether or not the sublimation of sexual energy can account for great artistic works, as Freud seemed to argue it does.

Although some insight into an artistic work can be gained using an archeological sublimation analysis, Ricoeur believes that the majesty of a truly great work cannot be contained by such a reductionistic, deterministic, and mainly tragic approach. He argues:

> If Michelangelo's *Moses*, Sophocles' *Oedipus Rex*, and Shakespeare's *Hamlet* are creations, they are so in proportion as they are not mere projections of the artist's conflicts, but also the sketch of their solution. Because of their emphasis on disguise, dreams look more to the past, to childhood. But in works of art the emphasis is on disclosure; thus works of art tend to be prospective symbols of one's personal synthesis and of man's future and not merely a regressive symptom of the artist's unresolved conflicts. (p. 521)

Notice Ricoeur's juxtaposition of concepts: *conflict-solution, dreams-works of art, disguise-disclosure, childhood-adulthood, analysis-synthesis, past-future, regressive-prospective,* and *symptom-synthesis.*

Conflict, dreams, disguise, childhood, analysis, past, regressive, and *symptom* are from the vocabulary of analysis, determinism, and reductionism, what might be termed the mostly tragic hermeneutics of suspicion. As necessary and helpful such a mode of inquiry may be, it leaves out crucial comic aspects of human existence. These aspects are hinted at by the terms *solution, works of art, disclosure, adulthood, synthesis, future,* and *prospective.* This vocabulary suggests the mainly comic hermeneutics of faith and hope.

Both faith and hope are windows to a realm of existence that the persons of modernity — although not Sayles and Kasdan — are reluctant to acknowledge, namely, the transcendent, with its emphasis on teleology (intentionality, freedom, and concern with future goals, ends, or purposes). Suspicion entails archeology and imminence; faith and hope entail teleology and transcendence. What are the implications of this tragicomic understanding?

To have faith is to believe or trust confidently, presumably in something that is not in our immediate experience. To hope is to wish for or desire something expectantly. John Sayles depicted a powerful tragically pessimistic illustration of the meaning of hope (and faith) in the way urban people's lives can be so oriented to the present by dispiriting life circumstances that all they do is claw out survival through any means possible, usually the cynical and brutal manipulation of others. The lack of faith in any societal institutions — including the family, education, religion, and government — and absence of hope for a meaningful future, lead to a tragic ending of madness and despair. Kasdan, on the other hand, comically, more optimistically, depicted persons who transcend violence and rampant alienation through their faith and hope in something beyond themselves. They treat each other as persons and thereby find meaning in otherwise tragic, meaningless, and menacing circumstances.

Faith and hope are future-oriented personal dispositions relative to what is beyond the immediately present, yet having powerful effects in the present. The hermeneutics of faith and hope, therefore, entails interpreting and finding meaning in our human condition in its nonimmediate, nonsensory, or nonperceptible aspects, and as it might be in the future. All of this concerns the transcendent — that which proceeds beyond or lies outside what we perceive in experience yet influences the way our experience gives rise to action.

Modernity is reluctant to deal with the transcendent because of its dictum that all legitimate knowledge is positivistic (from the Latin, *positivus,* formally laid down — that is, firmly anchored in measurable sense experience). In that regard, one of the meanings of transcendent is being beyond comprehension — vague or obscure. And vagueness and obscurity are precisely what modernity usually fears and judges realms beyond immediate sense experience to entail. We will never grasp the full meaning of ethics, however, unless we are willing to attempt to be clear about the transcendent and about the hermeneutics of faith and hope as a means of understanding transcendence. Levinas (1961/1969), for example, argues that we cannot know anything at all without the transcendent realm of the infinite, which "is the condition for every opinion as also for every objective truth" (p. 25). The infinite "is the common source of activity and theory" (p. 27). He also shows it to be, as we shall see, the source of ethics.

A related point briefly made here is that faith, entailing a venture into the transcendent, is part and parcel of the tragicomic human condition and of all our attempts to know. For example, in his writings on justice, Veatch (1986) argues convincingly for the necessity of faith moves to avoid the infinite regress inevitably encountered when a knower is pushed further and further back upon his or her assumptions. In addressing our search for reasons for an action being just or unjust, Veatch argues: "When we reduce the problem of morality to its most fundamental starting point — the basic assumptions with which we get an argument going — we are forced to posit a set of faith moves by which existence in a coherent, morally comprehensible world is possible" (p. 106).

Making faith moves and venturing into the transcendent is more than a necessary evil. Some might assert that it would be ideal if we could avoid transcendence and the need for faith, but we can't. Such grudging acceptance of the transcendent, however, ignores its positive contributions. Attempting to be clear about the transcendent is the only way to approach clarity about tragicomic human existence and ethics. In that regard, David Bakan (1966) accused the modern social and behavioral sciences of practicing *methodolatry*, systematic inquiry's version of idolatry, a topic that helps us understand what faces us in reflective-generative practice.

The locus classicus for idolatry in the Western intellectual tradition is the Old Testament account of Moses bringing down from the mountain the tablets containing foundational moral insights, only to find the people frivolously worshiping the golden calf. Idolatry names the irony of preferring the surface (gold) to ultimate concerns (Tillich, 1952). "Idolatry is to yield to the bribe of the manifest" (Bakan, 1966, p. 6). Methodolatry, then, is the worshiping of the surface — *method* — for its own sake, even if it keeps us from seeking the truth through probing ultimate concerns. Updating the Moses story, Abraham Kaplan (1964) recounts the modern parable of "a drunkard searching under a street lamp for his house key, which he had dropped some distance away. Asked why he didn't look where he had dropped it, he replied, 'It's lighter here!'" (p. 11). Preference for the methodological security of the lamppost over the willingness to search for the keys even though it means venturing into the darkness is methodolatry — operating according to what Kaplan calls "the Principle of the Drunkard's Search" (p. 11).

We must alter our methodological outlook in the behavioral and social sciences. We must transcend the principle of the drunkard's search and use a variety of methods, including those of the humanities, beyond those of positivism-empiricism, and we must open our theorizing to encompass all the phenomena that define the tragicomic human being, especially intentionality and freedom. Behavioral and social sciences that continue to practice methodolatry will fail to understand the meaning embodied in human action (Bruner, 1990).

Many academic disciplines, disenchanted with the failures of positivism-empiricism to deliver truly meaningful insights into the tragicomic human condition, have started to probe the transcendent and avowedly to enter the domain of spirituality — a domain that may or may not entail theology (Dokecki, Newbrough, and O'Gorman, 1992; O'Gorman, Newbrough, and Dokecki, 1995; Schneiders, 1989). The most basic meaning of spirituality refers to acknowledging and probing ultimate concerns. One's work may be said to have a spiritual dimension if it addresses the meanings and ultimate concerns embodied in tragicomic human action.

So far, I have hinted at the grounding of ethics in the nature of the person and in the transcendent, suggesting that modernity's penchant for method — particularly positivist science — gives an incomplete and possibly distorting picture of tragicomic human existence and the realm of ethics. In what follows, I develop a view of the person — an anthropology — that helps form the foundation for the ethical analysis needed in reflective-generative practice. I argue, first, that an understanding of the *face-to-face relationship* is necessary to establish the foundation of ethics for reflective-generative practice. Secondly, that an understanding of human existence as tragicomic and multifaceted — entailing the personal agent, the interhuman (the realm of the face-to-face), and the social — is required for a full and adequate address to professional life. These understandings lead us to the sociology of knowledge, which has important ethical and methodological implications for reflective-generative practice.

The Face-to-Face Relationship

Imagine a person you meet for the first time to accomplish a task of mutual importance. You may be enacting the roles of client and professional, or perhaps you are engaged less formally. You are close to and in front of her (or him) and are looking intently at her face — that is, you are face to face. What do you experience and how do you feel? You may get a general impression of her face and then notice particular features — her nose, her lips, her eyes. Perhaps it is the other way: feature after feature, then the whole. You may become aware of your own face — your nose, your upper lip, your eye glasses if you wear them. Perhaps your awareness shifts from her face to yours.

You probably perceive that she is reacting to your gaze and realize that you are reacting to her gaze, to her reaction to your gaze, and to your reaction to her reaction. Perhaps one or both of you show signs of embarrassment — shifting glances, nervous mouth movements. You may judge her attractiveness. You ask yourself how she is judging your face and what she is thinking and feeling.

Maybe you look into her eyes. Beyond the immediate facts of their color, placement, spacing, and shape, there is more in them than meets your eye. After all, the eyes are the windows to the soul, aren't they? Perhaps you begin to wonder about what she is really like — the life of her mind, her history and experiences, her likes and dislikes, her strengths and vulnerabilities. Perhaps you think about the life of your mind, your history and experiences, your likes and dislikes, your strengths and vulnerabilities. You may wonder if she is thinking and feeling the same as you are. You know one thing for certain, however; she isn't you. You are different persons. You probably have some similarities in background and experiences; but she is she, you are you.

The two of you speak, communicate using language, engage in discourse. Perhaps you recognize that each of you exercises a certain power over the other, for good or for ill. What kind of future interactions will you have? Is friendship or perhaps even love a possibility? Hatred and animosity? What are the future possibilities of this face-to-face encounter? If you really stop to think, the possibilities are endless, infinite. "The face is present in its refusal to be contained," says Levinas. "In this sense it cannot be comprehended, that is, encompassed" (1961/1969, p. 194). In encountering a person face to face, I encounter the other as a window on the infinite. The other may be similar to me in certain respects because of living in a common world. In a very fundamental sense, however, the other is "infinitely transcendent" (p. 194), radically[4] different from and thereby at least partially mysterious to me.

The otherness of the other is important, argues Levinas, because speech, language, discourse, and ethics arise in the otherness and difference revealed in the face. The other poses ultimate questions for me. I am unable to comprehend another person encountered face to face fully in my own terms because we are not the same person, and this has profound implications. The face-to-face relationship of two persons, as they reveal to each other through their difference the transcendent and the infinite, is the beginning point of our ultimate concerns. Not stopping at the surface of people but relentlessly pursuing the truth enables us to go beyond our usual attempts to translate the world completely into our own categories, to go beyond rendering the mystery of the other as if he or she is merely a copy of me, to go beyond using the other as means to my own ends. I am a unique person, different from every other, and the other is unique and different from me and every other. An initial ethical task is to honor this difference and diversity of persons wherever I encounter it, respond to its call to go out of myself into the transcendent, and thereby actualize my human development and enter into community.

The other, says Levinas, puts me in question. The other forces me to ask who I really am. He or she forces me out

---

[4] Although Bernstein (1992) agrees with Levinas on the importance of recognizing the difference between persons, he thinks, and I agree, that the word *radical* overstates the difficulty two pesons have in participating in each other's world and communicating.

of my complacency and safe harbor into uncharted waters, beyond my senses and immediate perception and understanding. Of course, I may, tragicomically, interpret the other's challenge to my self-understanding as threatening to me and my understanding of my world or, alternatively, as presenting to me an opportunity for growth and development. How will and should I respond? Will I welcome the other's challenge as an opportunity to develop humanly and enhance our mutual community, or will I respond defensively, even hostilely? The other "does not do violence to me, does not act negatively" (p. 197); rather, its structure is fundamentally positive and ethical. The other overflows me, exceeds my powers, and summons or welcomes me into the realm of morality and ethics. This overflowing into infinity, moreover, constitutes a call to expand my thinking and knowing beyond current capacity, although the infinite will always exceed the grasp of my thought and knowledge. Looked at in this way, the other encountered in the face is the root both of our desire to know the world and to act ethically in the world we come to know.

Levinas's phrase "does not do violence" is crucial. The face presents itself as sensible — able, in the extreme, to be negated, annihilated, murdered. "Murder alone lays claim to total negation," says Levinas (p. 198). But it also opens me to the transcendent, which is not subject to my power, that is, cannot be negated, annihilated, murdered. The naked face tragicomically communicates a person's extreme vulnerability. Since the sensible one is extremely vulnerable, I can easily harm, even kill, him or her. The other may physically resist me, and we *may* engage in armed struggle (war, at the societal level). We may engage in the all too human tendency to go to war, out of a fear-driven desire to defend ourselves from real or imagined threat or out of an imperialistic desire to exploit the weakness of the other. This is a societal ethical problem of perduring enormity.

But the human situation is tragicomic. The infinity of transcendence heralded by the face is basically and potentially more powerful than murder and war. If, in the beginning was the word, then the first word expressed by the face is, says Levinas, "you shall not commit murder." And the first word of our mutual discourse is "obligation," the ethical obligation of peace. We are ethically obliged to relate to others in a nonviolent, peaceful manner. "The epiphany of the face is ethical," says Levinas (p. 199), suggesting that if we give priority to what is primary in existence — the ethical, given by the transcendence of the infinite manifested by the face — and not to what is secondary — the imminence of the sensible world — then we will act morally. We will assume the obligation that emanates from the face-to-face situation. We will be nonviolent and peaceful and engage in discourse or dialogue, which results from and respects the freedom of persons encountering each other face to face. Moreover, the obligation we freely take on (*liberty*) before the face gives rise to discourse that manifests community (*fraternity*) and the demand for justice (*equality*). One can interpret developmental theory (e.g., Erikson, 1967) to suggest that precisely such discourse, enacted with liberty in a community (fraternity) of equality, is the condition for human development.

What does the other command? Actually, *we command each other* to be responsible to our mutual obligation of fraternity (community). Our responsibility is to recognize our obligation to respect and work for the fundamental equality of persons. We are to recognize the tragicomic — that each of us is simultaneously vulnerable and finite while manifesting the infinite, and that this paradox is central to the ethical call to enhance human development and promote community. All this suggests a metaphor, drastically stated, for the fundamental ethical choice facing reflective-generative practitioners (and the rest of us) — namely, seek peace, avoid war.

In a warlike relationship, the professional uses his or her unequal power position irresponsibly to treat the client, in win-lose fashion, as nothing but a sensible thing to be manipulated, coerced, and exploited for the professional's own purposes, even to "get away with murder." In a peacelike, caring relationship, the equality of a face-to-face encounter between client and professional enables both persons, in win-win fashion, to respect the uniqueness, *personal autonomy*, and vulnerability of the other and to engage in responsible discourse, characterized by *justice*, that will bring about human development and community. Professionals do not intentionally harm the client ("you shall not commit murder"), which expresses the ethical principle of *nonmaleficence*, and they strive to meet their ethical obligation to care for the client by addressing vulnerability in a caring and competent fashion, the ethical principle of *beneficence* — all within the context of the tragicomic human situation (see chapter 3 and Beauchamp and Childress [1994] for explication of the traditional ethical principles of respect for personal autonomy, nonmaleficence, beneficence, and justice).

The Ethical Spheres of Human Existence

Professional intervention entails, in terms derived from Farley's (1990) phenomenological approach echoed in the Introduction to characterize jazz, (a) the client and professional as persons — the *personal* sphere, (b) the interpersonal relationship between them — the *interhuman* sphere, and (c) the institutional context of this relationship of persons — the *social* sphere. The interhuman is primary, argues Farley, because it is the sphere of the face, and Farley's insight and its elaboration is the source for this section of the chapter.

The face is both the beginning and ending points of professional intervention. Using the metaphor of the experiment, it is the basis for both pretest and posttest: we look to the face in assessing the *is* of the immediate situation (pretest); the face influences the *ought* of problem-setting and problem definition; and we look again to the face to determine whether or not we have helped enable change — that is, helped lessen the *is-ought discrepancy* at the heart of professional intervention efforts (posttest). Why is this so?

The face issues a primordial summons, according to Farley, calling us to responsibility and commitment. This summons evokes the responses of compassion and obligation. The face as a universal transcends the differences among normative cultures and enmeshes us in a world of committed responsibility and compassionate obligation. We are summoned out of egocentrism into a caring relationship with another person who is suffering. Actually, all persons are suffering, because suffering is part of our tragicomic human situation. Ethics begins, therefore, in our existential condition, not as an arbitrary and relative construction of particular societies and cultures, although historical context does influence ethical particulars.

The ethical foundation of summons-response, moreover, is, using Farley's term, *tragic*, using my term, *tragicomic*. "*The most general feature of our human condition is its tragic character*," says Farley. "The term *tragic* refers to a situation in which the conditions of well-being require and are interdependent with situations of limitation, frustration, challenge, and suffering, . . . necessary conditions of creativity, affection, the experience of beauty" (p. 29, emphasis in original). This is not a gloomy, pessimistic picture of human existence, merely a complex and realistic one, again, tragicomic in my terms.

The arts, of course, provide many examples of the tragicomic interdependence of suffering and creativity. Robert Altman's film *Theo and Vincent* portrays it movingly in the life and early death of Vincent Van Gogh. The Clint Eastwood-produced film *Bird* presents the saga of jazz great Charlie Parker, who both improvised music as brilliantly as anyone who ever lived and died in his thirties "of everything." In both cases, creativity and suffering were tragicomically intertwined.

This intertwining of well-being and suffering suggests that we are, in Ernst Becker's (1973, p. 33) phrase, "angels who shit," as apt a characterization of the tragicomic as you will find. The young child discovers, at toilet training time, that the angelic and the excremental are interdependent. Could this wonderful and allpowerful creature that I am produce this smelly disgusting mess? Thereby begins what students of culture have learned — that all human culture is a tragicomic response to this paradoxical situation. I am simultaneously transcendent and determinate, and I am vulnerable in this transcendence and determinacy.

The Interhuman

The face is a phenomenon of the interhuman sphere of existence. In the interhuman, I encounter the other as a feeling, thinking, and behaving person. The other is a given in my world, "always already there [and] already intersubjectively formed" (Farley, p. 36), manifest to me in dialogue and empathy. The other is available to me in our shared interpersonal emotions, but is also a mystery, as we have seen in Levinas, the window to the transcendent and infinite.

Tragicomically, although the interhuman and its summons to compassionate obligation is there, as a given, prior to our conscious reflection on it, it can nonetheless be suppressed and put out of mind. We must continually strive to actualize its ethical potential. It is there, but we must continually work to sustain it. It discloses the other's and my own fragility, our vulnerability. And this vulnerability is central to ethics.

"Vulnerability is the capacity of a living creature to undergo harm," defined as "the frustration of the needs and desires of that creature and the pain and suffering that accompany that frustration" (Farley, p. 42). Suffering is interhumanly experienced because the face summons me and the other to mutual compassionate obligation. We are vulnerable because we are tragically imperfect, but this imperfection is the tragicomic origin of both obligation and incompatibility. There is an inevitable lack of total harmony among free and responsible persons.

The vulnerability manifest by the face in the interhuman challenges us ethically as free persons to meet our obligations to the other compassionately, despite incompatibilities that tempt us to stay within ourselves. If we freely choose to work on our own agenda and ignore, even manipulate, the other's suffering in order to achieve our own aims and desires, then we have violated our ethical responsibility. In the parlance of professional ethics, this is the dual relationship encountered in chapter 1. Although complete harmony of perspectives is impossible because of interpersonal incompatibility, if we fail even to try to be compassionate and meet our obligation to the other, we are unethical, we are evil more than tragicomic.

The interhuman, so structured and already there for us prior to thought and reflection, gives rise to a shared world in which social reality comes to be constructed. This shared world is partly given, partly developing, and partly perpetually negotiated and to be accomplished. The interhuman makes possible reciprocal perspectives and negotiated differences. We are called to work together in this shared reality to complete mutual projects and to ascertain the truth — in other words, to bring about community and human development. I return to the givenness, construction, development, and negotiation of social reality later in this chapter in considering the origin of the professions from the perspective of the sociology of knowledge.

It is important to note that the compassionate obligation to care for the other, summoned by the face, encounters a central aspect of the tragicomic human condition, says Farley, namely — our natural egocentrism. It takes courage to transcend our selfish agenda and to engage in mutual and reciprocal relations with other persons, especially to engage in appreciative caring. The beauty of the face as it manifests the transcendent, however, helps us recognize the comic aspects of life and fuels the courage that it takes to care. As tragicomic agents, however, we are free not to care for the other appreciatively, free, in other words, to refuse the ethical summons to caring issued by the face, free to be unethical in our professional and general lives.

In appreciative caring (I present an elaboration of the phenomenon of caring in chapter 3), the self is not totally sacrificed for the other. Rather, it contributes to the human development of both the one cared for and the one caring. The ethical choice here is not the either/or of the pure selfishness of self regard (self over other) versus the pure selflessness of other regard (other over self). Appreciative caring, the ethical challenge of the interhuman, is a matter of having the courage to engage in mutual regard — concern for both self and other as persons worthy of care and respect. Both refusing to be drawn beyond oneself (narcissistic egocentrism) and totally denying oneself (self-sacrificial altruism), therefore, are failures to heed the ethical summons of the face.

We must understand the interhuman in relationship to the other essential spheres of tragicomic human existence, the social and the personal. In Farley's analysis, these three spheres are interdependent, overlapping, and irreducible one to the other.

The Social

Knowing the self and others entails "an already formed sociality that contains institutions, languages, customs, and norms" (Farley, p. 47). The social is the realm of power, requiring us to be suspicious of its working and to be willing, tragicomically, to attempt to correct it where necessary. The ethical task is that of making the social world better — that is, criticizing and correcting oppressive abuses of power (I present elaborations of the concept of power later in this chapter and in chapter 3). The corruptions of power distort the social structures and processes that constitute society, the social world, and social systems. This suggests the importance of community psychology and other public policy-related interventions.

Of particular relevance to the ethics of reflective-generative practice is the role played by face-to-face communities in the social sphere. Professionals ought to promote such communities because they are the necessary social environments for enhancing human development. A community, for Farley, is a social grouping in which common purposes and aims are negotiated in face-to-face encounters. I would argue that the most basic "common purposes and aims" are human development and community.

Communities are enduring groups (the family, the neighborhood, voluntary associations, the church) that provide social support and resources for their members. They help enable persons tragicomically to deal with social vulnerability, which in the social sphere leads to incompatibility and suffering. The face-to-face community can serve as a model for the professional-client relationship.

Social incompatibility often entails alienation between the individual and the collectivity, the focus of much of Freud's writing. It also entails the unavoidable conflicts among individuals and groups in competition for society's scarce resources. But social incompatibility is not evil. "Rather, it bespeaks the intrinsic finitude and tragic structure of the social" (Farley, p. 59). Just as the interhuman sphere entails tragedy, so too does the social. The tragic is not the unethical. The tragic, however, makes being ethical a task to be mastered in the tragicomic struggle against the unethical corruptions that follow from our free choices as moral agents who make up social groups.

Social suffering takes many forms, says Farley, but of particular importance for our purposes is the suffering attendant on social evil. Social evil, the root of much unethical professional behavior, produces suffering that deprives others of their rights and of the humanity of the face. Society often calls on professionals to, in effect, nihilate clients, especially the deviant ones who threaten our understanding of our world — addressed again later in this chapter. Professionals, therefore, may fall into the ethical abyss of social evil to the extent that their interventions dehumanize and subjugate their clients. This happens, for example, when white male professionals invalidate the experience of women or members of ethnic minority groups by being grossly insensitive to their particular needs and perspectives (Abramowitz and Dokecki, 1977). It may also happen when professionals have sexual relations with their clients, as I explore further in chapter 3.

The Personal

As persons and agents, we are tragicomically passionate. We live in time, in an ever-moving present manifesting influences from the past and strivings toward the future — again the theme of transcendence and a hint of the importance of narrative to human meaning. "Human transcendence," says Farley echoing Levinas, "is the capacity to exist self-consciously in the face of discerned possibilities and to respond to situations in the light of what is discerned." It provides the "very possibility of human action and is what makes us moral, cognitive, and aesthetic agents" (p. 69). The resistance the world offers to us by virtue of our tragicomic condition necessitates that we expend significant effort in our actions, and it is our passions that fuel the effort necessary to achieve what we need and seek.

The deepest most desires that propel us through time, says Farley, are the *elemental passions*: They orient us to the three existential spheres of the interhuman, the social, and the personal, and they give rise to a variety of tragicomic actions and motivations. These elemental passions characterize each person. They are never fully satisfied, aim more at general states of affairs than particular things, oppose what resists them, and manifest natural egocentrism. They are, as I have termed it, tragicomic, not inherently evil; their willful corruption, however, entails the dynamics of human evil.

Evil, the domain of human existence that contains the willfully unethical, exists, says Farley, interdependently in the interhuman, the social, and the personal. From the perspective of the personal agent, human evil is *idolatry*, a major negative manifestation of our tragicomic life world, a phenomenon we encountered in the earlier discussion on transcendence. Idolatry's effect is the opposite of human development and community. Human development — the major positive manifestation of our tragicomic life world — can be understood as the growth and broadening of a person's experience over the life span. It entails both an increase in the amount of our experience (progressive differentiation) and changes in the ordering of experience toward coherent meaning (hierarchic integration). We come to experience more and more of our world more and more meaningfully. In George Kelly's (1955) terms, we chose in order to extend and deepen our understanding of the world.

Idolatry, on the other hand, constricts and diminishes our experience and our freedom. When we worship a surface thing as an idol, this idolatry "constricts freedom because it reduces the powers and dimensions of human reality. It invades and restricts personal being . . . and corrupts the elemental passions" (Farley, pp. 136–37). Paradoxically, then, we exercise our freedom in choosing to idolize the surface or mundane, only to restrict our freedom by being tied fearfully to the idolized thing. We thereby fail to respond to the transcendent ethical summons of the face. How does this happen?

Since the human condition is tragicomic (Farley's tragic), when our elemental passions lead us to attempt to achieve the unachievable, we suffer and experience frustration and anxiety. In effect, we put questions to the world but receive incomplete, unsatisfying answers. In George Kelly's terms, anxiety is being caught with your constructs down. This anxiety provoking and frustrating state of affairs leads us to believe that chaos hides at the core of reality. And chaos "is the one situation we human beings seem incapable of accepting" (Farley, p. 131), a phenomenon encountered again later in this chapter in the sociology of knowledge.

The intolerableness of impending chaos leads us to

respond with resistance. In an act of denial, we delude ourselves that the tragic and attendant chaos "can be avoided, tamed, managed, even defeated" (Farley, p. 132) and thereby deny our tragicomic imperfection and finitude. Resisting our finitude alters our relationship to both the mundane and the transcendent. We falsely come to believe that the merely *relative* satisfactions the mundane is capable of providing can miraculously satisfy as if they were *absolute* satisfactions. And when we make the relative absolute, we also confuse the infinite with the mundane. We come, in other words, to treat the mundane as infinite and the infinite as mundane. "In this deeper sense the dynamics of human evil is the dynamics of idolatry," says Farley (pp. 134–35). And it is precisely the dynamics of evil as idolatry that diminishes the freedom of the tragicomic human agent.

To the metaphorical tension between *war and peace* as basic to professional choice, therefore, we can now add *idolatry* as the metaphor for the unethical way of engaging in the client-professional transaction. Idolatry is to treat the other in its superficial manifestations, as a thing to be used for our own gain, not as a person worthy of respect and care. All of this undergirds and elaborates the current emphasis in ethics on respect for personal autonomy.

Levinas's and Farley's phenomenological analyses have helped provide a foundational understanding of the tragicomic human situation necessary for a full appreciation of the ethics of reflective-generative practice. Another critical foundational piece of the story entails the sociology of knowledge, a tale of the intertwining of knowledge and power.

The Origins of the Professions and Intervention: Managing Knowledge and Power

Power issues permeate institutional life and the professions. One of the most general ethical imperative regarding power is that we should use it to treat humans as persons, ends in their own right, not as things, the means to our own ends. This principle restates the Kantian rule of respect for persons and echoes the Judeo-Christian position that each person is made in the image and likeness of God, and therefore must be treated with reverence and respect. In modern parlance, we should empower persons (help them locate and develop their own sources of power), or stated negatively, we should emancipate persons from power that dehumanizes and depersonalizes them as things to be manipulated for the purposes of others.

Empowerment to help others become more self efficacious (*freedom to* pursue one's life projects) and emancipation to help others escape from the exploitive power of others (*freedom from* oppression), therefore, are challenges that face reflective-generative professionals. "How can I contribute to others' and my own liberation and emancipation?" is a central question. It leads us toward enhancing freedom by equalizing the societal distribution of power and promoting human development and the common good. In reference to the jazz metaphor, we should recall the development of jazz by African-American musicians in the context of, and often in response to, oppressive political, economic, and social conditions in American society.

Viewed societally, clients and professionals often function as relatively powerless pawns in an institutional chess game with high power stakes. As we shall see, society needs professionals to help serve institutional power needs. Professionals legitimate and delegitimate with their societally sanctioned authority and institutionalized power. Their reality-defining power is central to professional ethics. Analyzing it helps us to understanding both why all societies have had professions and how societal members experience resulting client-professional situations. As should be readily apparent, however, professionals' reality defining power is not necessarily Kantian or Judeo-Christian in respecting persons. Given our tragicomic human situation, it often runs counter to rather than promotes human development and the common good.

Alfred Schutz's (1967) sociology of knowledge framework, as elaborated by Berger and Luckmann (1966), the intellectual foundation of this section, helps us to discern the origins of professional intervention and its ethical imperatives. This aspect of our emerging reflective-generative framework complements the analyses of the immediacy of client-professional encounters and of the social realm presented thus far with the help of Levinas and Farley. Taken together, these analyses make clear that *ethical concerns are foundational for professional intervention,* not merely add-ons occasionally encountered in an otherwise technological endeavor.

Investigation of the origins of the professions and professional intervention profitably begins with the hermeneutics of suspicion. This attitude can be thought of as "normal paranoia," what might be called "situational paranoia." It leads one to ask penetrating questions about things ordinarily taken for granted. Early in my career as a clinical psychologist, I glimpsed the utility of judicious practice of the hermeneutics of suspicion. In the mid 1960s, I was serving as a consultant to a well-known and innovative therapeutic community in one the nation's best known mental hospitals. The head psychiatrist, a noted community treatment specialist, requested that meals be served on the ward, rather than in the large dining hall, to approximate homelike community conditions. It was a therapeutically reasonable request made by one of the hospital's respected and presumably powerful persons. But it was vetoed by the hospital's food service because food had never been served in other than the dining hall out of convenience and, therefore, never would. Stunned, I came to formulate a suspicious and tragicomic hypothesis: organizations devote much of their energy to the latent purposes of organizational maintenance and survival — in this instance, serving meals for the convenience of the staff. Less energy often goes to the manifest purpose of the organization — in this instance, helping persons with mental illness become well through the application of community intervention concepts.

This anecdote suggests that institutional life has manifest and latent functions — in effect, dual functions echoing the phenomenon of the dual relationship initially identified in chapter 1. The manifest functions may be more visible, but they may not be — in fact, often are not — more powerful in influencing institutional life. The tragicomic dynamics of institutional power are potent but far from obvious. This institutional subtlety suggests the view that reality is socially constructed, a construction intimately related to the societal distribution of knowledge and the consequent distribution of power. The knowledge-power equation suggests that knowledge — ordinary, scientific, and professional — has many functions, and although some of them may not be reducible to the exercise of power, the lens of power is nevertheless an essential analytic tool. In analyzing the ways in which we construct social reality and our knowledge of it, therefore, we should attempt to discern, with an appreciation for the tragicomic nature of the human situation, whose power and interests are at stake in particular institutional contexts. Berger and Luckmann's (1966) Schutzian sociology of knowledge is particularly helpful here.

Everyday life, argue Berger and Luckmann, is social: the person is always social. Even cloistered nuns, Trappist monks, and hermits live in a social world, if only in their thoughts as they meditate in their cells and caves full of imagined others from past, present, and future. Our tragicomic experience of the structure of social life entails participation in a social stock of knowledge. Shared symbols and language allow us to represent aspects of this knowledge of the social world to ourselves and others as we live our everyday lives. Knowledge is the medium of social exchange. It is like water to the fish and air to our lungs — absolutely necessary but often taken for granted.

We maintain, legitimate, and develop the institutional order as we communicate this social stock of knowledge to current and future members of society. As communicated in the course of socializing and educating children and performing activities of everyday life, knowledge is distributed differentially across persons and groups. No one person can know everything. Some persons know certain things, others know other things. All of us know more than any one of us. Every society, say Berger and Luckmann, has a distribution of knowledge.

In Emersonian fashion, if knowledge is power, then there is a connection between the distributions of knowledge and power. Each societal member participates in society's institutions by taking roles, thereby laying claim to some aspect of the distribution of knowledge (and power). A role is an enforceable guide for behavior: we expect those who assume roles — for example, that of a public official or of a professional — to behave within certain limits. We accord status and power when persons effectively enact these roles, and we exact consequences when they transgress their role limits.

Roles are the embodiment in knowledge and experience of the ways society institutionalizes and legitimates human conduct. When persons assume or are assigned roles, we believe they have knowledge of specific sectors of the societal stock of knowledge that empowers them to participate in the social world in prescribed ways relative to this knowledge. Thus, we accord educators, ministers, and psychologists status and power when they demonstrate that they know things that not just everybody knows and are able to act in accordance with their knowledge on behalf of their clients and society. But we are ahead of the story. We have yet to see where professions (e.g., education, ministry, and psychology) and professionals (e.g., educators, ministers, and psychologists) come from.

The social order with its social actors occupying social roles, say Berger and Luckmann, is an ongoing human production transmitted from generation to generation. It has both subjective and objective qualities, as we saw in chapter 1. It is simultaneously real and interpreted. We are born into an existing social order that we experience as palpable, real, and as if it has always been and will always be there. We are socialized into it through developing our portion of the social stock of knowledge and taking on particular role expectations, including that of professional in some cases.

We construct the social order, but our social world requires ongoing legitimation or justification. We come to experience it as real, worthy of attention, in need of interpretation, and, eventually, having moral-ethical force. A particularly important instrument of legitimation, say Berger and Luckmann, is the symbolic universe. This is society's theoretical tradition (or set of traditions), which organizes its diverse institutions and roles into a coherent totality. We experience a meaningful social world and our place in it. We may experience the symbolic universe as the American way of life, or our generation's way, or the way things are and should be done. It is the basis of the British "done thing" or of Spike Lee's exhortation to "Do the Right Thing." It provides the background for society's ethical understanding.

This social order legitimated by the symbolic universe is precarious. Although it provides a reasonably predictable social framework, we tend to experience it as always on the verge of disorder because of the presence of competing social realities embodied in puzzling and threatening persons and events. We experience a kind of social angst or existential anxiety (Kelly's [1955] notion of anxiety as being caught with your constructs down). "The institutional order, like the order of individual biography, is continually threatened by the presence of realities that are meaningless in *its* terms. The legitimation of the institutional order is also faced with the ongoing necessity of keeping chaos at bay" (Berger and Luckmann, pp. 103–4), as we saw earlier in Farley's analysis. Berger and Luckmann illustrated this precariousness-chaos phenomenon by recalling the national psychological crises attendant on the assassination of President John F. Kennedy in 1963. The controversy that continues to rage about the Kennedy assassination, almost thirty years after their book was published, recently fueled by Oliver Stone's *JFK*, demonstrates the urgency and potency of the need for continuing legitimation of the institutional order by "the most solemn affirmations" (p. 104). Today, we could mention the razing of the Berlin Wall, the 1992 Los Angeles riots, the 1994 Los Angeles earthquake, or the 1995 Oklahoma bombing. "Solemn affirmations" were indeed the order of the day, offered by the president and a legion of officials and media figures.

The omnipresent threat of disorder, chaos, and anomic terror — the experience of the social order's precariousness — is one of the phenomena that is foundational for social intervention, for the professions, and for the professional intervention role. Societal precariousness demands serious attention; therefore, society engages in what Berger and Luckmann call universe maintenance: we develop conceptual machinery — that is, mythological, theological, philosophical, scientific, ideological, ethical, and professional systems. And we empower certain people to preside over these conceptual systems and enact the universe maintenance roles that flow from them. Almost as a by-product of these bodies of knowledge, we create cadres of experts (shamans, ministers, philosophers, scientists, ideologues, ethicists, and professionals) and give them power to intervene in the social world to protect it from threateners. We do this to maintain and ongoingly to legitimate the symbolic universe. Professionals of various sorts are central actors in universe maintenance.

Symbolic systems (and those who purvey or embody them) that run counter to, contradict, or deviate from the prevailing symbolic universe threaten us. They signal the chaos lurking just beneath our ordinarily taken for granted social order. This suggests why the actions and apparent value systems of deviant persons, such as homeless persons, persons with mentall illness, and persons in the so-called underclass, among many deviant groups, threaten us so. We have difficulty in comprehending and dealing with the social reality these groups embody.

Alternative symbolic universes are embodied in the deviant persons found in all societies. Societies always encounter what Rhodes (1978) called the *deviance predicament.* This is the never-ending need to intervene in the situation of the ubiquitous deviant ones so as to remove or lessen the threat they pose to a society's prevailing values and way of life. The deviance predicament gives rise to what Rhodes (1972) called the *cycle of behavioral threat and community response.* Deviant persons threaten social values and the status quo. They require community response that removes the threat. In Freudian terms, threateners embody the id with its turbulent instincts, which must be opposed by forces embodying the superego as the repository of societal values and mores, and, not incidentally, power interests. The community calls on forces embodying the ego (e.g., professionals) to do the society's bidding by holding the threateners at bay and protecting the distribution of power through universe maintaining interventions.

The deviance predicament gives rise to a special form of universe maintenance. This is therapy, in its most generic sense, as a form of social intervention. Therapy helps "insure that actual or potential deviants stay within the institutionalized definitions of reality" (Berger and Luckmann, p. 112). Society sanctions therapists of many kinds — from witch doctors and shamans to psychologists and psychoanalysts. Society empowers these prototypical professionals to *diagnose* and *cure* deviants, to disabuse them of their alternative symbolic universes, and to return them to the safety of the prevailing symbolic universe and its moral-ethical order. We thereby preserve the prevailing distributions of knowledge and power. One societal root of the professions, therefore, is our need for a therapeutic function to preserve our safe harbor and keep terror and chaos at bay. Professionals tragicomically communicate and enforce societal values through their therapeutic interventions.

Another form of intervention, according to Berger and Luckmann, is nihilation, encountered earlier in Farley's thinking. This societally sanctioned action, performed by professionals and other societal actors, uses knowledge and various techniques to remove what is outside the prevailing symbolic universe. Nihilation takes two forms. First, "the threat to the social definitions of reality is neutralized by assigning an inferior ontological status, and thereby a not-to-be-taken seriously cognitive status" (Berger and Luckmann, p. 115). This is the pervasive phenomenon of preserving the existing distribution of power by assigning, for example, persons from minority groups the status of *nonpersons*, as in Ralph Ellison's novel, *Invisible Man*. We thus figuratively nihilate persons by turning them into nonpersons. Among the many powers society grants to professional persons is this tragicomic reality defining power, which can be either helpful or harmful to those who experience it.

In its second form, nihilation grapples with deviants in conceptual detail. "The final goal of this procedure is to *incorporate* the deviant conceptions within one's universe, and thereby to liquidate them ultimately" (Berger and Luckmann, p. 115, emphasis in original). Professional spin doctors are always interpreting deviant world-views in terms familiar to us so that we can comprehend and deal with them on our own terms. This is another example of the tragicomic power maintaining but potentially dehumanizing role that society asks professionals to play.

The picture I have been painting with Berger and Luckmann's help is of the professions as forms of social intervention (universe maintenance) exercising power decisively but conservatively. Society asks professionals to preserve the status quo against those who threaten current holders of power. And, indeed, many of society's intervention agents — psychologists, educators, and many other professionals — are conservative maintainers of the prevailing power structure, whether or not they understand this to be their function.

We must, however, never overlook society's need for social change and development. And here we encounter a tragicomic tension at the heart of many ethical dilemmas. On the one hand, "it is correct to say that theories are concocted in order to legitimate already existing social institutions" (Berger and Luckmann, p. 128) — a *conservative* function. We call on professionals to be, in effect, society's sanitation workers (those called on to justify the status quo) helping to keep society neat and clean on behalf of those who possess power. On the other hand, "it also happens that social institutions are changed in order to bring them into conformity with already existing theories" (p. 128). We demand, or ethically *should* demand, more from the professional role than conservation of the prevailing social world. Not only maintaining the status quo but also *fostering social change* is necessary for a society to survive, grow, and flourish in the interests of the human development of its members and thereby the common good.

Human development, then, requires both maintaining and legitimating the social harmony of stable communities and effecting meaningful, sometimes even revolutionary, social change. An important dimension of professional ethics is to acknowledge this tension between the need for societal legitimation and maintenance and the need for social change. The ethical challenge for the tragicomic reflective-generative professional is to get the right mixture, to manage the tension in pursuit of human development and the common good.

This tragicomic ethical tension between conservation and revolution seems always to be with us. For example, continental philosophy has argued about conservation-revolution extensively in what may be called the Gadamer-Habermas debate (Bernstein, 1983, 1986). Briefly, Hans-Georg Gadamer, the most important figure in twentieth century hermeneutics, has argued that tradition is necessary for knowing about the world and engaging in praxis to enhance freedom. In order to know anything, we know it through the lens of a particular historical, cultural, or intellectual tradition within which we engage in dialogue with members of our community. Jürgen Habermas, the leading contributor to the Frankfurt School's version of critical theory, has argued that tradition always oppresses us and curtails freedom because it interferes with free and uncoerced communication, critical theory's moral-ethical ideal.

I am persuaded of the importance of *both* dialogue within a tradition *and* the ethical ideal of free and uncoerced communication and that there is tragicomic wisdom in combining the Gadamer and Habermas positions. We must, à la Gadamer, be members of a tradition to know and change anything. We must be some place to move to another place. Traditions, however, are inevitably ambiguous — that is, they contain differing interpretations of key aspects of the tradition. Consider, for example, the well known differences between conservative and liberal Catholics or between the behaviorists and cognitivists in psychology. What is necessary to keep a tradition alive and developing, to avoid the heavy hand of tradition or the death of a tradition from premature hardening of the categories, is that there be, à la Habermas, communication and dialogue between members of a tradition that is as free and uncoerced as we can make it. We thereby can modify the old and construct a new reality (Tracy, 1987).

But pluralism and its attendant social fragmentation characterize our world (MacIntyre, 1981; Tracy, 1987). There are differing interpretations of key aspects of public life from tradition to tradition. Perhaps the most dramatic example we have today of radical plurality of interpretation is the conflict between the right to life and the right to choice views of abortion. Again, what is necessary for the public to achieve the common good is that we find some common ground for free and uncoerced communication between these different traditions.

The jazz metaphor is helpful once again. Gadamer embodies the top-down, structured, tradition-related aspects of the music. Habermas stands for the bottom-up, freely expressive, tradition-challenging forces necessary for artistic creativity. Without the structuring of the tradition, whatever music is made would be incoherent; without creative and innovative expression, whatever music is made would be mechanical, stilted, and decidedly not jazz. Thus, both in jazz and in the ethics of professional practice, the tragicomic challenge is to manage Berger and Luckmann's tension between conservation and revolution. The client-professional transaction, therefore, has potential both to preserve and to change aspects of the lives of the parties involved.

Given this social phenomenological understanding of the origins of ethics and the professions, we can now begin to elaborate the ethical position inherent in the model of reflective-generative practice. In effect, I will elaborate many of the theoretical and philosophical perspectives developed thus far through consideration of a number of professional concerns. Chapter 3 further develops the framework for reflective-generative practice through considering relationships with specific clients. Chapter 4 extends the story to the realms of community and public policy.

3

Further Elaboration of the Ethics of Reflective-Generative Practice: The Professional-Client Transaction

Psychologists often hold an advantage of power over the people with whom they work, especially when they are psychotherapy clients or students. They occupy a position of trust and are expected to advocate the welfare of those who depend on them.

When psychologists place their own needs and goals above those of consumers or when they lose sight of the fiduciary nature of their professional relationships, exploitation, faulty professional judgment, and harm to consumers can result. Ironically, the psychologists are often harmed as well. —Patricia Keith-Spiegel and Gerald P. Koocher, *Ethics in Psychology*

The profession has reached a consensus view regarding sexual intimacies with clients. That view is, "Don't do it. No matter what." There is a clear prohibition against the behavior. Engaging in sex with patients is wrong under any circumstances, it is unethical, and it places patients at risk for harm. — Kenneth S. Pope, Janet L. Sonne, and Jean Holroyd, *Sexual Feelings in Psychotherapy*

Professionals have authority to put me in jail, to hospitalize me, to excommunicate me, or in other ways to affect significantly the structures of meaning and of freedom in my life. — Karen Lebacqz, *Professional Ethics: Power and Paradox*

The reflective-generative practitioner's ethical task in the professional-client transaction is the pursuit of the client's human development and of community in our life together. This entails professionals relating face-to-face with clients in an intersubjective I-Thou (Buber, 1958) relationship. In other words, professionals should always and everywhere strive to treat clients as persons worthy of respect in their own right — and to promote community-like social conditions in which such mutual-personal relationships are encouraged. Ideally, there would not be even a hint of Buber's I-It mode of relating in which clients are treated as things — means to professionals' or any end other than meeting their human development needs.

Pursuit of human development and community, I assert, is the regulative ideal for professional practice, an ideal that should guide all aspects of practice and continually challenge the practitioner in all client-professional encounters.

I use the term *regulative ideal* to suggest that the pursuit of human development and community is *the* ethical course of action to pursue in every client-professional encounter — in effect, a prima facie duty, even though it is extremely difficult, nay impossible, to enact perfectly in any given encounter. In our tragicomic human condition, we inevitably fall short because of our imperfections as human persons and because of societal forces that pull us away from human development and community and toward problematic, selfish, and exploitive uses of power. In other words, there is an inevitable fusion of Buber's I-Thou and I-It modes of human relationship. Therefore, we inevitably treat each other both as persons and as things, in effect, being dual in our relationships with others (as we saw in chapter 1). We are called on to be ethical, however, we enact the professional task in a multifaceted, tragicomic world that presents us with inevitable ethical issues, conflicts, and tensions.

In the first part of this chapter, I focus on that form of dual relationship entailing professionals having sex with clients in psychotherapy, counseling, and other helping relationships. I adopt this focus as a means of developing further a reflective-generative ethical frame-work. This phenomenon is a microcosmic and particularly troublesome instance of the more general ethically multifaceted challenges facing the professional who pursues the regulative ideal of attempting to promote human development and community. By focusing on sex with clients as an instance of the inevitably competing demands of professional life, however, I in no way attempt to excuse this behavior. In Pope et al.'s words opening this chapter, "Don't do it. No matter what," a reasoned and widely accepted proscription regarding a very serious professional matter.

The Use and Abuse of Power: Professionals Having Sex with Clients

Dual relationships are highly problematic, and professionals should be ever vigilant of the potential for abuse of power within their tragicomic transactions with clients. Accordingly, most professions, especially those concerned with mental health and human development, have clear and strict ethical prohibitions against many forms of professional-client dual relationships, especially those involving sex with clients. Yet such activities persist. Practicing therapists treat so many victims of sexual encounters with former therapists that they often use the term *epidemic.*

The phenomenon of professionals having sex with clients seems to be rampant in the United States, having increasingly come to public attention since the early 1970s. Virtually all the professions, both inside and outside the mental health arena, are implicated, and the media are full of news stories and dramatized accounts of the sexual activities of the clergy (including high level and well-known religious leaders), teachers, physicians and dentists, psychologists and psychiatrists, lawyers and politicians, and the like. The portrayal of *L. A. Law*'s lecherous lawyer, Arnie Becker, has made the phenomenon a virtual cultural commonplace. The making of movies portraying sex between therapists and clients, such as *Final Analysis, Mr. Jones,* and *Prince of Tides,* which have featured some of our most popular media figures, also suggests that the topic is on our collective cultural mind.

Consider this passage from Stephen White's (1991, pp. 2–3) novel, *Privileged Information:*

> I tell him I have fantasies of seeing him outside the office. He says, you have a pattern of enticing men to respond to you sexually. I translate: you're saying I try to get men to come on to me? He nods, stays formal. It's not necessary to repeat that pattern with me, he assures me, this relationship is different. Given your past, he says, it shouldn't surprise either of us that you are trying to generate sexual intimacy between us. But in this relationship, it's something we can work to understand, not a destructive pattern to act out again. . . .
>
> I hear him, but I don't hear him. Why?
>
> Because I need him. Because he wants me. I have to respond to that. I must. He's nurtured me, en-couraged me, helped me discover me. . . . I don't want him to leave me.

The speaker here is a woman in therapy with a man, the typical arrangement in dual relationships entailing client-therapist sexual relations. As is common, and even desirable in psychoanalytically oriented psychotherapy in which analysis of the transference neurosis is the order of the day, the client has sexual fantasies about her therapist — the phenomenon of transference. Although she fantasizes that he needs her, the passage doesn't indicate whether or not he has fantasies about her — countertransference. But it shouldn't surprise us if he does, and let us assume that, in fact, he does.

Apart from the particular dynamics of certain forms of

psychotherapy, this passage suggests a universal feature of client-professional relationships, namely, a *power differential in favor of the professional.* A client enters a relationship with a professional experiencing a need that the professional is believed competent to address. The situation entails a *necessary* status differential, based on the professional's presumed training, experience, skills, and special knowledge. Unless the professional is believed to know something the client doesn't, there is no reason for the professional relationship in the first place. Since knowledge is power, the knowledge differential is also a power differential. The professional's tragicomic power may be used caringly and ethically, where the intent is the mutual promotion of human development and community and thereby the common good, or unethically in manipulative or coercive fashion, where the intent is to give priority to his needs over those of the client.

The client in the passage candidly speaks of her dependence on the power of the therapist: "I need him. . . . He's nurtured me, encouraged me, helped me discover me. . . . I don't want to leave him." An immature and incompetent therapist could mistake her sexual interest in him as personal, only coincidentally related to the therapeutic relationship. He could feel flattered and respond in kind, thinking that he would be innocently (and ethically) engaging in a sexual relationship between consenting adults. But he would thereby be mistaken and would, in fact, be acting unethically — engaging in, at the very least, an unwitting abuse of his professional power. A blatantly unethical (*evil* in Farley's terms) therapist, of course, could freely and manipulatively take advantage of his power advantage and her dependence to, in effect, rape her, that is, have sex with her against her will. He would be operating against what we presume her will would be if she were freed from the power of the professional relationship.

But our client is fantasizing about an apparently mature, competent, and ethical therapist. He recognizes that she is not sexually attracted to him apart from his professional status: "He says, you have a pattern of enticing men to respond to you sexually. I translate: you're saying I try to get men to come on to me? He nods, stays formal." He, so to speak, interprets the transference in order to help her gain insight into her situation. Moreover, he seems to resist the temptation and structures the situation in a competent, caring, and highly ethical fashion: "It's not necessary to repeat that pattern with me, he assures me, this relationship is different. Given your past, he says, it shouldn't surprise either of us that you are trying to generate sexual intimacy between us. But in this relationship, it's something we can work to understand, not a destructive pattern to act out again."

Stephen White, himself a practicing clinical psychologist, has packed a great deal of ethical insight into this brief fictional passage. He portrays the complexity of the client-professional transaction and the inevitability of tragicomic power-related factors and motives operating within it. This mixed-motive feature of professional life, often leading to the abuse of professional power, requires further analysis, including analysis of the societal construction of gender. In chapter 1, I argued that one of the foundational barriers to ethical professional practice is that of the powerful traditional constructions of gender. I elaborate this ideological observation by means of an analysis that begins in human personality.

One enduring insight of psychoanalysis is that each person, despite his or her biological sex, has both masculine and feminine psychological characteristics. Over the course of personality development, these characteristics are blended in unique ways for each person. To oversimplify, it is useful to view the *normal* male as having ascendent masculine relative to feminine characteristics in his personality, with the *normal* female in like fashion having ascendent feminine characteristics. Especially for Jung, the major issue concerns the *degree* of dominance or ascendence of one set of gender characteristics relative to the other. If a man is so exclusively masculine that his masculine side completely dominates or submerges the feminine, and he cannot "get in touch with" his feminine side, this is a sign of immature psychological development and potential psychopathology. A similarly problematic case is that of a woman in whom the feminine totally dominates the masculine. For Jung, the mature and *healthy* state of affairs is one in which ascendence does not mean total domination, in which a man can recognize his feminine side and a woman her masculine side. At this level of personality development, male therapists who have sex with their female clients can be characterized in terms of immature psychological development and potential psychopathology, although this in no way excuses their clearly unethical conduct.

This psychoanalytic gender-based analysis of individual personality development may be extended to the societal level. Different societies and different historical periods display different masculine-feminine blends in their values and modes of societal organization. David Bakan (1966), as we have seen in chapter 1, has argued that modern

Western society has come to be heavily imbued with masculine (agency) values — enacted through manipulative power and mastery — to the virtual exclusion of feminine (communion) values — enacted through more caring forms of power. We must rectify this exaggerated tragicomic situation, says Bakan, by *mitigating agency with communion* — in effect, mitigating masculine values with feminine values. This wouldn't entail a war between men and women, and the goal is not to replace male dominance with female dominance, which would merely be another extreme version of the either/or (and incidentally agentic/masculine) logic and power strategies that have characterized our societal norms and mores. Rather, the goal is to help society be in better balance, to express the tragicomic more humanely, through encouraging the expression of *both* masculine *and* feminine values, an expression that would not take the form of a shouting match but of a dialogue or a conversation. In this way, men and women as individual persons would be enabled to develop more fully, and societal development would also be enhanced. Moreover, the resulting state of affairs would be more conducive to ethical professional practice than the masculine value position that has traditionally dominated the social-institutional context surrounding the professional-client transaction, one that leans precariously more to the tragic than the comic. This gender-based analysis begins to identify personality and cultural factors at the heart of professional practice and many other aspects of our society.

Ethical Discernment[1]

It is helpful to continue the development of the ethics of reflective-generative practice with an actual client-professional transaction in a very different domain, early intervention. In a recent paper, Michele Sokoly and I described and analyzed this typical, at least in form, client-professional encounter:

> Robbie Jones, 6-months-old, was born 2 months premature and given only a 5% chance of surviving. His parents are trying to be realistic about Robbie's limitations, are conscientious about finding the best care available for Robbie, and are doing all they can to help him develop to his fullest potential. They began an early intervention program when Robbie was 4-months-old and are seeking the help of many health care and early intervention professionals. They realize there are no guarantees about the future: No one can say with accuracy what Robbie will be like in a year, and the five-year or ten-year outlook is highly uncertain.
>
> Recently, a neurologist informed the parents that Robbie most likely would not develop cerebral palsy. The mother's predictable reaction of elation, however, elicited disparaging comments from the neurologist. "Mrs. Jones, you must remember that cerebral palsy is just a small part of the coin! We need to concern ourselves with Robbie's mental capacity," the mother reported him saying.
>
> Robbie's mother experienced a profound sense of frustration and being misunderstood. She tried to appreciate the neurologist's position — he wanted her to realize that much more than cerebral palsy was involved; but she felt he did not have an accurate sense of what this news really

[1] Certain material in the remainder of this chapter appeared in somewhat altered form in Sokoly and Dokecki (1992).

> meant to her and her family. One of their major fears — that her son would have to be "strapped in a wheelchair with his head hanging down and his arms and legs straight out" — was apparently disconfirmed. Although she understood that this was but one dimension in the complete picture of Robbie's handicaps, she still viewed it as an occasion to celebrate: "When someone gives a parent a white piece of paper, paints it all black, and someone else comes along and throws a little white spot on it, a parent is going to take that spot and milk it for all it's worth." In evaluating her exchange with the neurologist, Robbie's mother concluded: "You just have to consider the source. After all, he is a professional." (Sokoly and Dokecki, 1992, p. 25)

Let us use this case to explore the process of *ethical discernment* and related matters.

Briefly, discernment is the capacity to evaluate a situation, find out its morally relevant features, and decide why these features are important. Discernment yields a tragicomic vision of our obligations and decisions pursuant to action. Before acting, however, there is problem setting. In setting the problem, we choose to focus on this rather than that aspect of a situation as a problem, frame the reality of that problem, and define the problem so that it is amenable to intervention. In effect, discernment addresses the *is-ought discrepancy*: We assess what *is* in the current situation, evaluate the is in terms of what *ought* to be. And we plan an intervention that we hope will reduce the *discrepancy* between is and ought, all in the context of the tragicomic human situation.

More broadly, understanding the professional-client transaction from the standpoint of reflective-generative practice entails: (a) defining and interpreting the intervention situation in light of, among many factors, rules and duty-based morally relevant features and professional role expectations, (b) examining the character of the professional, and (c) analyzing the structures of power that influence interventions in actual situations of professional practice (Lebacqz, 1985). Let us explore each of these dimensions of ethics.

Situations, Rules, Duties, and Professional Role Expectations

Robbie's mother was frustrated because she felt her family was treated as a "case number." She experienced the neurologist as evaluating the situation in such a way that he had a skeptical view of her ability to understand the implications of the child's condition. Although he might have discerned that an ethical rule governed the situation, giving rise to a duty to give the family a "realistic" picture of Robbie's limitations, he did not seem to discern an equally important rule and attendant duty: to respect the autonomy of the family and its values in the context of its community.

An essential aspect of ethics entails evaluating situations to determine the operation of timeless (and placeless) rules that require duties. One reason for a rule is to facilitate good consequences for the community. As with Robbie's story, however, just which rule applies in a given situation is often difficult to discern. The extreme view of this ethical ambiguity, situation ethics (Fletcher, 1966), is that there are no absolutely applicable, timeless, and placeless moral rules and duties except, in Skinnerian fashion, to maximize positive consequences in particular situations. The ethical literature is replete with debates between those arguing the primacy of rules (deontologists) and those who claim that only situations and consequences matter (certain of the consequentialists).

Lebacqz (1985) helps us cut through the debate over whether ethics is purely situational or situation-independent and rule-governed: "Both situations *and* rules are involved in every ethical decision. . . . All rules — or norms — are written *for* situations. . . . Thus, there is always a situation built into every definition of a rule" (pp. 22–23). Moreover, "morality is not simply a matter of calculating consequences. The nature of the human community is such that certain kinds of behavior are required to keep us human. . . . Morality . . . is also a matter of adhering to the structural requisites for human community" (p. 22). In effect, ethics exists to enable the establishment, maintenance, and development of community pursuant to human development and the common good (elaborated in chapter 4).

Before proceeding, I must make a crucial distinction, namely, the one W. D. Ross made between *actual* duties and *prima facie* duties. As Frankena (1963/1973, p. 26) explained Ross's position:

> What is actually right or obligatory is what we actually ought to do in a particular situation. About what we actually ought to do in situations of life, which often involve conflicts, . . . there are and can be, Ross admits, no rules that do not have exceptions. "Every rule has exceptions," that is, every rule of actual duty has exceptions. But there still may be and are, Ross contends, exceptionless rules of prima facie duty. Something is a prima facie duty if it is a duty other things being equal, that is, if other moral

> considerations did not intervene. . . . Accordingly, Ross suggests that one can formulate a number of rules that hold without exception as rules of prima facie, though not actual duty; it is always an obligation one must try to fulfill. But it may on occasion be outweighed by another obligation or rule of prima facie duty.

Thus, we have, for example, a prima facie duty to tell the truth (Bok, 1978), but we may decide to lie in order to deceive someone who intends to harm our child. Truth telling, however, is thereby in no way diminished as an ethical obligation by our decision to honor the competing ethical obligation to protect the innocent from harm.

Ross's distinction between prima facie and actual duty requires that we discern our ethical responsibilities carefully and sensitively, but with common sense. We must simultaneously understand our professional ethical obligations and recognize that they obligate (or don't obligate) in particular contexts. In Piagetian terms, we must be able to *decenter*, to recognize the moral force of rules and attendant duties, from one perspective, and of situations in their particularity and historical context, from another perspective. Rules and their attendant prima facie duties, therefore, constitute a general ethical framework that obligates us to make this rather than that choice in the transaction between the framework and the situation.

What can we say about the content of an ethical framework so understood? Ross's list of prima facie duties includes, among others, being beneficent (doing good), being nonmaleficent (not doing harm), and being just (working toward an equitable distribution of goods and evils). Lebacqz (1985) added respecting the autonomy of persons to this list.

Beauchamp and Childress's (1994) classic position in biomedical ethics combines all of these in proposing (a) *respect for autonomy*, (b) *beneficence*, (c) *nonmaleficence*, and (d) *justice* as the most meaningful and defensible set of ethical principles. They have guided professional practice and much of the rest of social interaction in the Western intellectual and moral tradition. This list seems broad, sensible, and useful. Much of what I have written thus far can be understood as a specification and elaboration of the principle of *respect for the autonomy* of persons — in short, the duty to treat all human beings as persons not as things, not being idolatrous in our dealings with them, treating them in peaceful rather than warlike fashion, and respecting them as ends in themselves not as means to our own ends. Much of what follows in this chapter about caring also relates to the principle of autonomy. Beyond autonomy, codes of professional ethics are typically heavily imbued with the principles of *beneficence* (do good) and *nonmaleficence* (do no harm). In its most basic form, the principle of *justice* entails the notion of distributive justice as equality of treatment (treat like cases alike and different cases differently). This seeming truism is not as simple as it appears, however, since not just any likenesses and differences but *morally relevant* ones must be discerned in the domain of justice. These morally relevant similarities and differences are "ones that bear on the goodness or badness of people's lives" (Frankena, 1963/1973, p. 51). Central are the concepts of needs and abilities.

Ethically, treating people in relation to their needs and abilities requires us to discern "whether doing so helps or hinders them equally in the achievement of the best lives they are capable of" (Frankena, p. 51). Further, the argument is not that persons are equal in endowments and capacities, because they clearly are not, but that "we ought prima facie to make proportionally the same contribution to the goodness of their lives, once a certain minimum has been achieved by all" (p. 51). I have been arguing throughout this book that the goods to be promoted, the harms to be avoided, and fairness in distributing these consequences in meeting our obligations to be beneficent, maleficent, and just entails, at base, human development and community. And in the tragicomic professions, at the heart of dealing with these consequences is the issue of professional roles.

Professional Role Expectations

In Robbie's story, the neurologist was presumably guided by the duties of respecting the autonomy of Robbie and his family, doing them good, avoiding doing them harm, and being just in dealing with them. But what actually happened? In effect, he gave his opinion, not facts, about the imprecise term *cerebral palsy*, and he reprimanded the mother for responding to it. As a result, she perceived him to be insensitive to the family's value system and as having little faith in her appraisal of the situation. She viewed him as treating their situation actuarially as a *case* — a thing needing quantification — not as relating to family members as persons. She viewed the neurologist as not respecting their autonomy, not doing them much if any good, doing them some harm, and treating them unjustly in trampling on their rights and sensibilities by a misguided use of professional status.

Among the bases for the *case number* approach is the phenomenon of professional role expectations. We think about our obligations in terms of our roles and develop notions of how we should act around others. "Roles provide a link between factual statements about what the situation is and normative assumptions about what the actors ought to do" (Lebacqz, 1985, p. 36) — again, the is-ought discrepancy. The questions, then, are: What are the role expectations of professionals and clients? What does each person expect from the other? What should we do?

Empowering and enabling clients in today's world require a fundamental reassessment of professional roles (Schön, 1983). Schön describes two very different models of professional roles: Model I (technical rationality) and Model II (reflection-in-action).

Technical rationality is the received view in modern institutional and professional life. In Model I, the major professional role is problem solving. Problem setting, the "process by which we define decisions, ends and means" (Schön, 1983, p. 39), is typically overlooked. A danger clearly inherent in this Model I approach is arbitrarily cutting, in Procrustean fashion, the practice situation to conform to professional knowledge — precisely what occurs when professionals apply an objectifying *case number* approach. The professional assumes the role of the expert, the one who knows all. The expectation is that clients will passively and docilely comply with the professional's advice. Therefore, Model I describes the traditional treatment-focused, top-down approach to interventions. In this version of the professional role, the professional has virtually all the power and all the answers: his or her role is to "fix" the individual client. Model I recognizes only part of the total picture represented by the jazz metaphor.

In contrast, *reflection-in-action* (Model II) entails reframing both the professional's and the client's role expectations. Model II calls for *complementarity*: The client and the professional enter a partnership that involves joint exploration of the situation. The professional has some expertise yet realizes that this knowledge is incomplete without the unique perspective of the client. This version of the professional's relationship with the client "takes on the form of a reflective conversation, where the reflective[-generative] practitioner tries to discover the limits of his expertise" (Schön, 1983, p. 300) instead of imposing predetermined knowledge upon the client.

The Model II reflective-generative practitioner enters transactions with clients possessing some expert knowledge and a theory of intervention. Unlike the Model I professional, however, the reflective-generative practitioner does not assume the traditional expert role. Instead, there is a reflective relationship with the client that involves exploring multiple perspectives and sharing responsibility for problem-setting and problem-solving. The client-professional partnership "incorporates recognition of the autonomy of those being served but also includes solidarity with them" (Lebacqz, 1985, p. 57).

Movement from the more typical Model I to Model II requires changes of perspective on the part of both professionals and clients. Tables 3.1 and 3.2, adapted from Schön, show the dimensions of these changes. They depict the changes in outlook required in the tragicomic professional's move from Model I "expert" to Model II reflective-generative practitioner, and in the client's move from the traditional Model I contract to Model II's reflective-generative covenant.

The contrasting professional perspectives on the client-professional transaction depicted in Table 3.1 suggest the need for significant, personally demanding change. Model I's all-knowing, objectively distant, and status-conscious role, one mostly blind to the tragicomic dimension of the human situation, would be shifted to Model II's appreciation for the limits of one's knowledge, connection with the client as a person at both intellectual and feeling levels, and relation with others in a more genuine, less status-directed fashion.

From the client's perspective, the change from Model I's traditional contract to Model II's reflective-generative covenant also requires significant, personally demanding change (Table 3.2). Many clients may be intimidated by reflective practitioners. They will have been socialized into a role of having faith in professionals and wanting them to guarantee security, being unquestioningly compliant, and expecting unerring professional expertise. A relationship with a professional entailing client participatory involvement, interdependence, and discovery will require some getting used to, and this in turn will require the tragicomic professional to be willing to engage in mutual learning and exploration with the client. It should be obvious that changed modes of professional education will also be necessary.

Two concepts come to mind in considering needed changes in client and professional role expectations, *partnership* and *shared responsibility*. "Partnerships are valued over paternalistic approaches," argue Dunst, Trivette, and Deal (1988, p. 9), "because the former implies and conveys

Table 3.1 Contrasting Professional Perspectives

Model I *Expert*	*Model II* *Reflective-Generative Practitioner*
I am presumed to know, and must claim to do so, regardless of my own uncertainty.	I am presumed to know, but I am not the only one in the situation to have relevant knowledge. My uncertainties may be a source of learning for me and for them.
Keep my distance from the client, and hold onto the expert's role. Give the client a sense of my expertise, but convey a feeling of warmth and sympathy as a "sweetener."	Seek out connections to the client's thoughts and feelings. Allow his respect for my knowledge to emerge from his discovery of it in the situation.
Look for deference and status in the client's response to my professional persona.	Look for the sense of freedom and of real connection to the client, as a consequence of no longer needing to maintain a professional facade.

Adapted from Schön (1983, p. 300)

Table 3.2 Contrasting Client Perspectives

Model I *Traditional Contract*	*Model II* *Reflective-Generative Covenant*
I put myself into the professional's hands and, in doing this, I gain a sense of security based on faith.	I join with the professional in making sense of my case, and in doing this I gain a sense of increased involvement and action.
I have the comfort of being in good hands. I need only comply with his advice and all will be well.	I can exercise some control over the situation. I am not wholly dependent on him; he is also dependent on information and action that only I can undertake.
I am pleased to be served by the best person available.	I am pleased to be able to test my judgments about his competence. I enjoy the excitement of discovery about his knowledge, about the phenomena of his practice, and about myself.

Adapted from Schön (1983, p. 302)

the belief that partners are capable individuals who become more capable by sharing knowledge, skills, and resources in a manner that leaves all participants better off after entering into a cooperative arrangement." This emphasis on partnership is complemented by Moroney (1986), in *Shared Responsibility*, who makes the concept of need central to his analysis of family social policy. He illustrated his notion of shared responsibility with a marvelous negative object lesson, worth quoting here at length, which is reminiscent of Robbie's story. While on a visit to the United Kingdom, Moroney:

> accompanied a local authority social worker carrying out a survey of handicapped persons. An elderly couple, the husband 80 years old and disabled from a stroke, the wife caring for him despite severe arthritis, was asked in the course of the interview what needs they had and what problems the local social services agency might help them with. By any number of standards, the couple had many professionally defined needs. They lived in a second story flat with the toilet in the backyard. The apartment was heated by a single fireplace and three space heaters. They were able to move about with difficulty but were visited by their neighbors. The couple told the social worker that they would like some assistance. The wife pointed to a large tree outside the bedroom window and said that they were worried that a large overhanging branch might strike the window and break it. If this were to happen in the winter, they might freeze to death. Neither she, her husband, nor the neighbors could do anything about it, and she wondered if the social worker could arrange to have the branch cut off. The professional response was not atypical: "That's fine, but let's talk about your real needs." (pp. 155–56)

In this and Robbie's story, the clients had a keen understanding of their needs. The professionals, however, were enacting a role and assuming a character that made them insensitive to their clients. The topic of professional roles, with attendant rules and duties, leads us to the critical issue of professional *character* and what it must embody, *caring*.

Character and Caring

Another critically important aspect of ethics involves character. A reflective-generative professional must ask not only "What am I to do?" but also "Who am I?" Actions over time must somehow be a whole, a narrative that makes sense and has coherence. The questions from this *virtue ethics* perspective become: What should the reflective-generative practitioner be like? What should the professional's life story be? Virtue ethics and the use of narrative are necessary complements to my mostly social phenomenological and action philosophy approach because they add a lifespan developmental perspective and go to the core of what reflective-generative practitioners must bring with them into professional situations, in the form of personal characteristics and virtues, in order to promote human development and community.

Codes of professional ethics serve several purposes, perhaps the most important one being to provide an ideal of professional life — in effect, the outline of a narrative depicting the nature of expected professional virtue — that is, the way professionals ought to comport themselves (Lebacqz, 1985). This ideal typically suggests that professionals should be fair with clients, competent and honest in their dealings with them, and not take advantage of them. These characteristics point toward three virtues central to professional life, *trustworthiness*, *prudence*, and, especially, *caring*.

The *trustworthy* reflective-generative professional person deals with issues at the very deepest level. This role implies the ability to perceive the client's system of meanings, to understand the intervention situation from the client's perspective, and to respect that perspective while working on the client's behalf. It means earning clients trust and sharing responsibility with them so they may maintain, or come to gain, power over their lives.

Related to trustworthiness is *prudence*, the ability to make competent decisions in real-life situations. It allows "letting the truth of real things determine what we do" (Lebacqz, 1985, p. 104). Prudence entails discerning good reasons for engaging in interventions through a process of perceiving the situation accurately, deliberating about it wisely, deciding what to do, and acting on that decision. The prudent reflective-generative professional can make the right decision by inviting clients to assume an active role in defining their problems and exploring avenues for intervention.

Particularly key to professional ethics is *caring*, an enduring mode of interpersonal virtue that promotes growth and development of the persons involved. For professionals to care, they must not only have expertise and knowledge about another person, but also self-awareness that allows them to evaluate whether what they are doing helps or hinders the human development of the other. They must, argues Mayeroff (1971, p. 13), "know who the other is, what his power and limitations are, and what is conducive to his growth." They must know and respond to the other's needs based on an accurate assessment of their own tragicomic strengths and weaknesses. To care for the other, the professional must be "*with* the other in his world. He must be able to see from 'inside' what life is like" (p. 42). Caring professionals treat each situation as unique and allow the "other's growth to guide what [they] do, to help determine how to respond and what is relevant to such a response"

(p. 7). Both these ideas are inherent in the role of the reflective-generative practitioner who trustworthily and prudently, albeit tragicomically, approaches clients as active partners in a growth-producing process, rather than as patients (literally, *passive ones*) who need to be "cured." If patients are passive ones, then perhaps clients as active ones might whimsically be called *actients.*

The Phenomenology of Caring

Let us take a phenomenological journey into the realm of caring, based heavily on Mayeroff's[2] (1971) analysis. Think of yourself as a caring person face to face with a person in need of care, as in the chapter 2 scenario. This cared for person summons the best in you, challenges you to discern her or his needs and to participate in helping meet these needs — although you may choose to ignore the summons.

When you care meaningfully, first, you intend to and are successful in helping meet persons' fundamental need for human development — that is, their need to grow — to respond to their life challenges in the context of a healthful and decent quality of life; to broaden their experiences; to develop and enlarge their realms of meaning; to actualize their potential; to be the best that they can be; to be generative. Second, you require a nurturing and supportive community to meet the many challenges facing those who choose to care in a sustained and meaningful

---

[2] Milton Mayeroff's *On Caring* has become a locus classicus on the topic. And I adopt much of his analysis here in order to develop this crucial dimension of reflective-generative professional life.

fashion. Community here should be understood as a social grouping that promotes human development. Not just any social grouping is a community in this sense. Indeed, one that hinders human development would be an anticommunity (chapter 4).

Caring is helping a person grow — helping promote a person's human development. It potentially characterizes many kinds of relationship, such as that between parent and child, wife and husband, husband and wife, two friends, teacher and student, therapist and client, physician and patient. And although there may be differences among these types of relationship, if they qualify as caring, they have a common pattern that entails going beyond merely knowing and relating to a person on the surface to a deeply personal level of tragicomic experience.

When you care, on Mayeroff's view, you enact a common pattern in which you are with and experience another person both as part of you and apart from you, and needing to develop humanly. Devotion characterizes your response to the cared for person, and her or his need gives direction to you caring actions. Interdependence not independence, dependence, or codependence best characterizes this part/apart relationship. Your ability to foster the other person's human development affects your own well-being and human development. You feel needed by the other person to grow, and you need the other's growth as a condition for your own growth and development. Thus, in caring, both the cared for person and the person caring grow and develop.

If, however, you choose to care for the other person *primarily* because you want to grow — that is, if you selfishly put your own needs before those of the other — you not only are not caring but are using the other as a means to your own ends, treating the other as a thing to be used for your own purposes. The often heard reason for entering a caregiving profession that it will help the professional to grow and find meaning, therefore, is problematic. Caring enables you to grow, *if* you intend your caring actions primarily to benefit the person cared for. This seems paradoxical, but it is essential to understanding caring's truly interdependent nature and to avoiding exploitive, dependency-inducing, or codependent relationships.

You help other persons to grow — and you in turn grow — through a process of enabling them (a) to care for other persons beyond themselves, (b) to identify or create their own domains of caring, (c) to care for themselves, and (d) to take responsibility for their own lives. Growing, for its part, entails learning, understood not as the accumulation of facts and skills but as enlarging one's scope of understanding by increasing one's experiences and integrating them into one's meaning system. Growing also entails becoming self determining — breaking away from slavish conformity, choosing one's values, making one's own decisions, and taking responsibility for them. Moreover, learning and becoming self determining occur within relationship, not in social isolation.

Our understanding is incomplete without specifying what the caring person must be like and do — in other words, the ingredients of the virtue of caring. Again following Mayeroff, these ingredients include alternating rhythms, patience, honesty, trust, humility, hope, courage, and perhaps most importantly, knowing.

Caring is not a linear process. It involves *alternating rhythms.* These rhythms are many and varied, and they include moving back and forth between doing (sometimes doing nothing) and experiencing and evaluating the results of your doing, and between taking a broad and a narrow perspective on the person cared for, yourself, and your caring actions.

Since you ground caring in the uniqueness of the persons cared for, you have *patience* to allow them to grow in their own time. There are times to act and times to wait. Waitful caring, however, is not passive but actively chosen, because that is what the moment requires. You also are patient in tolerating confusion. Someone once facetiously defined genius as the patience to delay making a decision in a confusing situation until the last possible moment before chaos sets in. Finally, you are patient with yourself in giving yourself time to master the challenges of caring.

As a caring person, you are *honest* with yourself and with cared for persons. You view the parties in the caring transaction as they are, not romanticized or glorified. Not only do you not lie, but you actively embody the truth by living authentically and "ringing true." As a tragicomic agent, you are willing to admit mistakes and take steps to correct them.

As a caring person, you *trust* your own caring capacity and trust cared for persons' capacity to change. Trust here implies your willingness to take risks, to enter unknown realms as the caring situation demands it. In addition, you are a trustworthy trustee — you can be trusted not to abuse power and take advantage of your caring position. This means sharing responsibility with cared for persons so they may maintain, or come to gain, power over their lives.

The *humility* entailed in true caring is multifaceted. It entails your willingness to admit what you don't know and to learn more about the caring process and the persons involved in it, including yourself. It means, as we have seen, not caring primarily to meet your own needs and not abusing your power. It means recognizing your limitations, but, as Mayeroff points out, it doesn't preclude your taking pride in caring well done, caregiving that results in human development.

Hope is crucial for caring. Since you are realistically humble, you are not presumptuous, but neither are you despairing about your ability to care meaningfully and effectively in challenging circumstances. Hope, however, is active not passive waiting; it entails the expectation that the future is full of possibilities to be actualized through your caring actions and the actions of the cared for person. Recall the hermeneutics of hope from chapter 2.

Caring requires the related virtue of *courage.* This courage relates to trust. It entails your willingness to enter unknown realms, founded on the tragicomic wisdom gained from past experience, the accurate understanding of the present, and the informed expectation of future possibilities.

Although caring may seem to reside mostly in affective or attitudinal domains, perhaps its most important ingredient is *knowing* — knowing that, knowing how, knowing both directly and indirectly, knowing both generally and specifically. You know who the cared for person is, her or his needs, strengths, weaknesses, also your own needs, strengths, and weaknesses. You know the most appropriate ways of responding to her or his needs to influence growth. Moreover, it is crucial to know the nature of the narrative you are constructing and enacting.

The Professional Narrative and Caring

I can best illustrate the connection between caring and narrative in professional life by describing a demanding, but ultimately much appreciated, assignment I require in a course on ethics for human development professionals. I suggest to students that, by virtue of their human development-related major and emerging professional interests, caring is central to their lives. I have them read and analyze Mayeroff's *On Caring* and use it as a lens for viewing where they have been, where they are now, and where they are going. I suggest that growth, understood as learning and becoming more self-determining, is integral to the human developmental process of becoming *generative.* Generativity is an achievement, an ongoing developmental task and the culmination of the developmental process. It leads people to be strong — that is, capable of making progress in ethically and meaningfully, albeit tragicomically, meeting life's challenges. Generativity, I maintain, has two coordinates — time and space.

Temporally, generative persons live in a world in which past, present, and future are dynamically interrelated. We live in a constantly moving *present* infused with traditions, memories, and influences from the *past* — what Freud knew so well — that is oriented intentionally and teleologically to a *future* filled with possibilities, purposes, ends, goals, and projects. Over time, a life characterized by caring will come to evidence a reasonable degree of certainty complemented by faith in the order of things, intelligibility with an appreciation for life's tragicomic mystery, a feeling of satisfaction with life, and a psychological sense of community.

I suggest to them further that, *spatially*, generative persons are ecologically situated, related to and respectful of the environment, natural and social. We live in a complex ecosystem where an appreciation for the interdependence of persons and their interdependence with other species and with the physical environment should characterize our actions, our ethics, our professional interventions, and our public policies. This constitutes a transactional-ecological outlook on our relationship to the environment. Thus, we are generative when we tragicomically construct and enact a narrative that manifests an appreciation (a) that we come from prior generations, are "in place" in our present lives, and have a duty to generations yet unborn, and (b) that we have a responsibility for the quality of the environment we occupy. The generative metaphor for our temporal existence is the *parent-child or teacher-student relationship*; *spaceship earth* as viewed from the Apollo moonshot provides the generative spatial metaphor. When we are temporally and spatially generative, our life has meaning. In other words, caring manifests the tragicomic by helping us create meaning in life, enabling us to lead a generative life.

Caring is an ongoing process of mutual enhancement of development that occurs in the ever moving present. The pattern of actions over time, however, not every particular action, must produce developmental movement toward generativity if there is really caring going on. *No development, no caring.* Given our tragicomic human situation, there may be dry spells when change is elusive. A general failure to influence development, however, should be a signal that understanding of the cared for person is inadequate and in need of revision or expansion. This demand for affecting development — enhancing the personhood and generativity of the one cared for — makes caring challenging.

I ask the students to reflect on their lives in light of these ideas (they may, of course, reject Mayeroff's and my formulation and offer an alternative of their own that helps them make sense of who they are as emerging professionals). I ask them to write a personal narrative in three parts: (1) *Past* — What key people and experiences in their lives to date have led them to be committed to caring as human development professionals? (2) *Present* — How do they see the university and their current major as embodying (or not) the ideal of caring? (3) *Future* — Can they discern how caring might be relevant to their future lives, both personal and professional, and what obstacles to being a caring person they might encounter in their particular professional worlds (helping services, public policy, law, business, and the like)? In effect, I ask them to make explicit the narrative structure of their emerging lives as reflective-generative practitioners. I ask them to reflect on the origins and future of their character and virtue.

The character of the tragicomic professional, therefore, plays a crucial role in client-professional transactions. What remains an issue, however, is how to promote caring character development and role expectations within the tragicomic institutional structure of society and in the structure and design of particular client-professional transactions and associated service delivery systems, topics that require return once again to exploration of the uses and abuses of power.

Further Considerations of Professional Power

The distribution of power, as we saw in chapter 2, is central to professional ethics. Society vests professionals, by virtue of their role, with authority. Professional power is "legitimated and institutionalized power" (Lebacqz, 1985, p. 113). Professionals do not simply have the power to fix a problem. They also define its reality. There is potential for distortion depending upon the way professionals use their tragicomic reality-defining power.

As tragicomic agents, argue Craig and Craig (1973), we exercise two very different forms of power depending on whether we relate to others as objects (directive power) or as persons (synergic power). *Directive power* is used by professionals who typically operate as Model I experts. They use their expert power to exercise control over the client. In doing so, they make the client dependent and powerless: "Directive power dehumanizes people because it makes them less sensitive to the fact that they cause the results of their actions" (p. 61). It reduces their belief in their own self-efficacy. Directive power, however, is the sort of power embedded within the structures of society. If we approach clients from this unfortunately typical use of power, we will rarely enable them and participate in their empowerment.

In contrast to directive power, *synergic power* suggests a very different view of professional power. Synergic power is "the capacity of an individual to increase the satisfaction of all participants by intentionally generating increased energy and creativity, all of which is used to *co-create* a more rewarding present and future" (Craig and Craig, 1971, p. 62). Operating from this model, clients are partners, colleagues and allies with whom professionals join in a cooperative relationship, as in Model II reflective-generative practice. Synergic power grows from trust and prudence and is caring. Its ultimate goals are to enhance people's senses of autonomy and interdependence that grow out of working together, to enhance people's view of themselves as capable of affecting their own and others' destiny, and to enhance people's view of others as capable of working together. Synergic power counters the traditional view of the professional as controlling expert, and it is this type of power that caring tragicomic professionals would employ as reflective-generative practitioners to enhance clients' human development and self-efficacy.

This concept of synergic power also relates to the societal distribution of power. Professionals must "seek to share power and redistribute it" (Lebacqz, 1985, p. 131). Yet there is a complex tragicomic paradox in notions such as empowerment and liberation. If professionals assume that their role is to empower or liberate clients, they may be operating paternalistically (Riger, 1993). Empowerment and liberation sometimes become directive when they imply that clients passively receive empowerment from professionals. The professional's use of power, therefore, must involve synergic efforts, wherein the client and the professional achieve levels of human development greater than either one alone could reach. Professionals, however, are tragicomic and thereby are never able to be fully synergic in their exercise of power.

Returning to Robbie's situation, it probably stretches the issue to call his neurologist unethical. He apparently intended his remarks to promote the good of the parents by making sure they did not develop unrealistic expectations for their child. The transaction with the family, however, was not particularly caring and of questionable validity and effectiveness. Unlike the prudent, trustworthy, and caring professional, he was unaware of the family's perspective. Consequently, the transaction resulted in frustration rather than development. Instead of communicating that he was a partner who was on the family's side, he struck the family as callous and insensitive, operating as Model I's technically rational expert with all the answers.

The Model II professional in Robbie's situation would not ask, "What can I do for this client?" but rather "How can I liberate and emancipate my client and myself?" Synergic rather than directive transactions with clients have a much greater chance of addressing their real needs and priorities, equalizing the distribution of power, and promoting human development and self-efficacy.

In Robbie's story, the family perceived the professional structures as entailing the exercise of directive power. The traditional role of the physician is to cure — to give patients directions about what to do to improve their conditions. With a child like Robbie with developmental disabilities, however, there is no "cure," no one prescription that will heal all ailments. Robbie's mother thought the neurologist did not make this distinction. Operating directively, he offered his evaluation of the child's condition — "It is highly unlikely that Robbie will develop cerebral palsy" — predicting with certainty the child's very uncertain future development. When she reacted positively to this news, she experienced the neurologist as seeking to direct her to a *realistic* assessment of the situation, emphasizing deficits and ignoring strengths, rather than understanding the family's value system. The mother and the professional did not jointly explore the problem; instead, she saw him as controlling the balance of power and knowledge by virtue of his professional status. They didn't relate as two persons (in a *we-relation*), and she experienced the relationship as lacking support and personal sensitivity.

The We-Relation and Client-Professional Communication

For synergic power to operate, we must recognize and enhance a type of relationship other than a paternalistic one. I refer here to the *we-relation*, a concept described by Alfred Schutz and expanded by, among others, Gibson Winter (1966). The we-relation extends chapter 2's analysis of the face. It entails interdependence of self and other as persons, not things. It involves "being conscious of the other by grasping the other's meaning" (Winter, p. 104). Meaning is manifest in the *personal projects* people choose to enact. Personal projects entail the goals and intentions that motivate people. They are the overarching schemes or plans that give shape to our lives. Projects take the form of the narratives we enact. They are what get us up in the morning and give direction to our strivings. The work of the tragicomic professional, therefore, is to explore and understand, by communicating with the client within the professional-client partnership, the nature of the client's projects; the task is not to impose meaning by the exercise of directive or coercive power. In effect, this analysis suggests that a basic aspect of the ethics of reflective-generative practice entails tragicomic human beings transacting as persons ("we") not as things, and that the key to understanding projects lies in client-professional communication.

The reflective-generative practitioner seeks to create situations approximating the ideal of "uncoerced consensus and nonmanipulated understanding and agreement" (Forrester, 1983, p. 238), the ethical standard for evaluating social arrangements in the spirit of Habermas's critical theory (Geuss, 1981). This ideal relates to the concept of synergic power and Model II reflective practice in emphasizing working together to formulate professional action, not imposing interventions upon clients. It also provides a means of coming to know the client's situation, which is central to the caring transaction.

Briefly, this critical outlook attempts to identify obstacles that impede communication and prevent clients and professionals from jointly exploring client projects and meanings. According to Forrester (1983, p. 236), explicating Habermas, claims to the validity of what "speakers and listeners . . . say and hear" must be considered. Listeners evaluate four claims in what they hear: (a) truth — the existence of some aspect of social reality; (b) legitimacy — the appropriateness of what they hear in the context in which they hear it; (c) sincerity — whether they believe the speaker means and intends to say what he or she is saying; and (d) clarity — the "comprehensibility and coherence" of what is being said. Acceptance of these communicative claims has pragmatic results. The claim to truth engenders belief, legitimacy engenders consent, sincerity engenders trust, and clarity engenders attention. We should believe, consent to, trust, attend to, and thereby comprehend what another communicates. On the other hand, when these claims are distorted, as they inevitably are in the tragicomic world, misinformation and manipulation may result, and our task is to correct or minimize these distortions in pursuit or human development and community and, thereby, the common good.

Summary and Conclusion

The ethics of reflective-generative practice is in the spirit of Lebacqz's (1985) work. She is one of the few ethicists of the professions to attempt to integrate most of the major ethical traditions: situation ethics, consequentialism, phenomenology, deontology, professional ethics, virtue ethics, and social/ideological ethics. And what have these ethical traditions told us so far about the ethics of human development professionals?

For the tragicomic reflective-generative practitioner, ethical issues arise within concrete professional situations as experienced by the involved persons. These situations, however, exist in historical and institutional context and have professional roles, rules, and duties as defining aspects. Human development and its problems are not exclusively matters of either the person or the environment but their transaction — the fit or lack of fit between a person's capacities and environmental demands. We must have the capacity to evaluate a situation, find out its morally relevant features, and decide why these features are important.

Discernment yields a vision of our obligations and decisions pursuant to action and problem setting. In setting a problem, we focus on a particular aspect of a situation as a problem, frame the reality of that problem, and define the problem so that it is amenable to intervention. This entails the is-ought discrepancy.

Reflective-generative practitioners, as inheritors of the Western intellectual and moral tradition, incur four primary situated obligations: respect for personal autonomy, beneficence, nonmaleficence, and justice. Moreover, we should realize that the client and the tragicomic professional enter a partnership of shared responsibility that involves joint exploration of the situation. We have some expertise, yet this knowledge is incomplete without the unique perspective of the client. We should have a reflective relationship with the client that involves exploring multiple perspectives and sharing responsibility for problem-setting and problem-solving.

Among the virtues central to the tragicomic reflective-generative practitioner's life are trustworthiness, prudence, and caring. Living as a trustworthy trustee entails perceiving the client's system of meanings and understanding the intervention situation from the client's perspective. It means sharing responsibility with the clients so they may maintain, or come to gain, power over their lives. Living as a prudent professional entails arriving at good reasons for engaging in interventions through a process of perceiving the situation accurately, deliberating about it wisely, deciding what to do, and acting on that decision. We attempt to make the right decision by inviting clients to assume an active role in defining their problems and exploring avenues for intervention. Caring is a mode of interpersonal relationship in which we treat clients as persons, not things and thereby promote the growth and development of the persons involved, professional and client alike, and help them become generative. It requires a nurturing and supportive community to care in a sustained and meaningful fashion.

Caring reflective-generative practitioners have tragicomic power. We do not simply have the power to fix a problem but also to define its reality. The kind of power we should try to exert is synergic power, which deals with the client as a person in order to promote human development, not directive power, which deals with the client as a thing to be used for our, not the client's, purposes. More generally, we should seek to share our power and to help effect an equal distribution of power throughout the society. We should seek to liberate, emancipate, and empower our clients (and ourselves) — without assuming that power is ours to dole out as we see fit, a decidedly directive and dependency-inducing posture.

Reflective-generative practitioners should explore and understand, in partnership with the client (the "we relationship"), the nature of the client's world. The task is not to impose meaning by the exercise of directive or coercive power. The key to developing such an understanding lies in client-professional communication, according to the ideal of uncoerced consensus and nonmanipulated understanding and agreement. Clients and professionals should believe, consent to, trust, and attend to, and thereby comprehend what they communicate, within the context of the tragicomic life world.

In the final chapter, I revisit many of the concepts developed so far in pursuit of a tragicomic community-oriented ethics, an ethics that addresses the inadequacies of the individualistically oriented ethics that has tended to characterized professional practice until now.

4

Reflective-Generative Practice and the Ethics of Community: Toward the Caring and Competent Community

You cannot use the moral vocabulary and consistently deny the force of ought, and you cannot remain within the social commerce of the community and abandon the moral vocabulary. — Alasdair MacIntyre, *A Short History of Ethics*

Ethics and ethical language can be regarded as part of the process whereby, as members of a community, we moderate our impulses and adjust our demands so as to reconcile them as far as possible with those of our fellows. . . . The only context in which the concept of 'duty' is straightforwardly intelligible is one of communal life — it is, indeed, completely bound up with this very feature of communal life, that we learn to renounce our claims and alter our aims where they conflict with those of our fellows. — Stephen Toulmin,

The Place of Reason in Ethics

If we call the harmonious interrelation of agents their 'community,' we may say that a morally right action is an action which intends community. —John Macmurray, *Persons in Relation*

Solidarity in a community (be it a smaller, larger, or world community) is necessary if peace is to reign and if persons are to be capable of leading at least satisfactory and fulfilling lives. Solidarity depends on a community's recognizing that community itself must be a transcendent goal. To maintain community means to do those things which help individuals within the community to flourish and grow; to maintain the flourishing of individuals means to do those things which maintain, strengthen, and solidify community and ultimately allow it to evolve and thrive. — Erich H. Loewy, *Freedom and Community: The Ethics of Interdependence*

We suggest that a theory adequate for promoting a

sensible approach to child development in this society should have as one of its major rationales the nurturance of caring. The rationale we propose . . . for national attention to human development . . . calls for the creation and support of a *competent and caring society.* — Nicholas Hobbs, Paul R. Dokecki, Kathleen V. Hoover-Dempsey, Robert M. Moroney, May W. Shayne, and Karen H. Weeks, *Strengthening Families*

The first opening quote (MacIntyre) is the core of the argument *for* ethics as rational (entailing assertoric knowledge and good reasons) and *against* relativistic and individualistic emotivism. The second (Toulmin) advances the argument that reason has a place in ethics only in the context of community, and that the very function of ethics, with its associated notion of duty, is to make community possible. The third (Macmurray) draws the conclusion that ethics fundamentally concerns community from the argument that human beings are fundamentally interdependent and connected personal agents rather than independent and alienated thinking individuals. The fourth (Loewy) is a recent account of ethics based on the interdependence of human development and community, and the actions that ought to be taken to enhance them. This account is reminiscent of a position colleagues and I developed in the context of value-oriented public policy analysis, as stated in the fifth and final quote (Hobbs et al.). We issued the call for a competent and caring society, what I call in this book, a *caring and competent community.*

Reflective-generative practice is grounded in these positions: it has as first principles human development and community and, thereby, the common good. Reflective-generative practitioners tragicomically, caringly, freely, and rationally intend to achieve these first principles as the primary goods internal to their practice and to give priority to them over external goods such as money and self-aggrandizement through the abuse of professional power. The common good giving shape to this vision is the caring and competent community. Elaboration is in order.

Persons-In-Community[1]

Warlike and idolatrous action, as we have seen, are destructive and ethically problematic modes of relationship, professional and otherwise, corrosive of both the person and the community. In that regard, Macmurray (1957, 1961) analyzed the crisis of the personal, modernity's inability to understand the fullness of tragicomic human existence and address it ethically. Macmurray's thought forms the basis the opening sections of this chapter.

Macmurray argues that two modern predicaments constitute this crisis of the personal: the mistaken priority given to thought over action — *the theoretical predicament,* and the equally problematic priority given to the individual over

[1] Certain material in this chapter appeared in somewhat altered form in Dokecki (1992).

the social — *the egocentric predicament.* We can address the theoretical predicament by arguing, à la Macmurray, that the person is fundamentally doer, actor, or agent *(ago,* I act), not thinker (*cogito,* I think). We can address the egocentric predicament by arguing that the person is preeminently socially interdependent rather than isolated. Persons are, in other words, *agents-in-relation.* So understood, we can begin to grasp the fullness of tragicomic human existence as practical, moral, and ethical. This understanding also suggests the outlines of a comprehensive and integrated methodology for knowing persons-in-community, a crucially necessary aspect of ethical professional practice. A professional person's practice should begin with the question, "How can I know what I should do?" This question places knowledge in the service of action, theory in the service of practice. Moreover, asking what we *should* do emphasizes the ethical dimensions of practice.

Reflective-generative professionals join with Macmurray in a modern Copernican revolution, substituting I do (*ago*) for I think (*cogito*), thereby standing us on our methodological head. Browning (1991), in the spirit of Macmurray, also opts for *ago* in preferring a practice-theory-practice logic to *cogito*'s theory-practice-theory approach. It is not that we don't think, because obviously we do. Thinking, however, is subsidiary to doing or acting — more precisely, both thinking and doing are forms of doing — in effect, two sides of the same action coin. Moreover: "We know existence by participating in existence. This participation is action" (Macmurray, 1961, p. 17). The resulting view of the person as practical self addresses the theoretical predicament, since theorizing (thinking) becomes comprehensible only in the context of acting. The professional, then, is a tragicomic actor trying to address the is-ought discrepancy inherent in professional situations. Theory is not valid unless it contributes to lessening this discrepancy. Theory does not justify practice; rather just the opposite: Practice is the reason for theory and the arena for its testing and validation.

Consistent with Levinas's and Farley's positions presented in chapter 2, Macmurray (1961), with Buber, asserts that the personal relationship of self and other is the ground of human existence. The self is You-and-I, and the other is You-and-I. In other words, selves are persons in relation, and personal existence entails personal relations. Further, personhood, as we have seen, requires communication as its founding relationship. Communication, moreover, entails language, which is human and personal, not organic or mechanistic. The person, on Macmurray's view, is *hierarchically and emergently organized at the mechanistic, organic, and personal levels.* Organism emerges from mechanism; person emerges from organism. This hierarchic arrangement, however, in no way implies that one level can or should be reduced to any other. Elaboration of Macmurray's distinction is in order, first at the level of the human being, then at the societal level.

The Level of the Human Being

The mechanistic human being, on Macmurray's view, is part of the material world and can be known deterministically (mechanism implies determinism) through categories such as cause-effect and mechanical action — in other words, through physical science methods. The organic human being is part of the living world and can be known through systems categories such as differentiation and integration, continual change and becoming, and teleological goal directedness — in other words, through biological science methods. The personal human being is part of the interpersonal (intersubjective, interhuman) world and can be known through categories such as consciousness, freedom, and intentionality — in other words, through human science methods.

In the practical world of person as agent and as valuing ethical being, knowledge is in service of the practical: Knowledge exists for action, and action exists for the sake of community. Moreover, persons ought to intend community: "We may say that a morally right action is an action which intends community" (Macmurray, 1961, p. 119).

At this point, we must make three observations regarding the ethics of community. First, the relational development of persons is not usefully understood using the bipolar construct of dependence-independence. Although we start life as dependent infants, human development through community results not in "independence, but a mutual interdependence of equals" (Macmurray, 1961, p. 66). The developmental task, therefore, is movement from immature dependence toward *mature interdependence* (see Loewy, 1993; Waterman, 1981).

Second, the family is the model for the personal world. The metaphor of the atomized rugged individual who requires agreement to a social contract before entering social relationships is misguided. Social relations among persons in groupings such as the family precede the formation of social contracts (Rawls, 1971, among others, provides an alternative view).

Third, "equality and freedom are constitutive of community; and the democratic slogan, 'Liberty, equality, fraternity,' is an adequate definition of community — of the self-realization of persons in relation" (Macmurray, 1961, p. 158). Thus, rather than having to choose between either liberty or equality, liberty or fraternity, or equality or fraternity — choices often presented in social philosophy and public policy analysis — we should pursue all three simultaneously since they are interrelated and mutually reinforcing. I return to these matters in a later section.

The Societal Level

As the person is hierarchically and emergently organized at mechanical, organic, and personal levels, argues Macmurray, so is the community. In that regard, we must distinguish between society and community. The term *society* refers to both mechanistic and organismic levels of social relations; the term *community*, however, should be reserved for the personal. A brief and schematic presentation of Macmurray's social categories helps explain and elaborate this distinction relative to a variety of longstanding conceptual categories.

The *mechanistic society* is egocentric (individualistic), is based on the negative emotion of fear, entails impersonal social relations (as in Buber's I-It), and seeks private interests. It faces the moral problem of achieving cooperation in the face of individuals resisting each other (the many) and competing for power. It attempts pragmatically to adapt means to ends through technical reasoning and operates according to a morality of law (and contract) backed by force to achieve obedience. Further, the *mechanistic social order* is liberal, humanistic, and individualistic, with intellectual roots in Roman law and Thomas Hobbes. It is the atomistic and contractarian society, and its major shortcoming is a tendency to produce alienation in its individual members.

The *organic society* is also egocentric (individualistic), is also based on fear, also entails impersonal social relations, and also seeks private interests. It faces the moral problem of integrating particular social relations into the whole social system (the one) in automatic and functional fashion. It attempts to maintain the social system through dialectical reasoning, entailing the development of the whole through the contrast of opposites, and operates according to a morality of good form to achieve orderly functional relations of each to all. The *organic social order* is imbued in romanticism and has intellectual roots in ancient Greek society and Jean-Jacques Rousseau. Organic society's major shortcoming, according to Macmurray (1961), is its tendency to become totalitarian, with the social whole submerging the individual, as in Hitler's Germany and Stalin's Russia.

In contrast to these forms of society, the *personal community* is heterocentric (not egocentric or individualistic), is based on the positive emotion of love (not fear), entails personal (not impersonal) social relations (Buber's I-Thou), and seeks the interests of the other (not exclusively the self). It faces the moral problem of overcoming fear-based hostility by love. It attempts to create and maintain community and friendship through practical reasoning and operates according to a morality of love and friendship to achieve the community of persons in relation (the one and many). The *personal community's social order* has its roots in the Judeo-Christian tradition, and, because it submerges neither the social (as in the mechanistic) nor the individual (as in the organic), it avoids both the alienated individual and the totalitarian state.

The personal community, on Macmurray's (1961) view, implies both the mechanistic and organic forms of society. In that regard, although each level has its distinct characteristics, they are interrelated in our daily lives, in effect, forming a tragicomic web. In our social world, says Kirkpatrick (1986, p. 205), explicating Macmurray, "the individualism and power relations of contract, the functional subordination within an organic whole, and the intimacy of heterocentric love all have a place." But the place of each level must be understood hierarchically — that is, in the "community of persons, there will be a hierarchy of levels of relationship, the lower ones serving the overarching and controlling higher ones. These lower levels [mechanism and organism] will serve as the infrastructure of community" (Kirkpatrick, p. 12). Thus, societal considerations of power, economic efficiency, distributive justice, and politics — features of the mechanistic and organic infrastructure — have a necessary place in the community.

Table 4.1, which is derived largely from Macmurray, summarizes the discussion thus far of the individual and societal aspects of the human situation. It suggests answers to key questions from the perspectives of the root metaphors (Pepper, 1942) — basic images of the world — of machine, organism, and person/agent.

Table 4.1 Analysis of Persons-in-Community

	Root Metaphor		
Question	*Machine*	*Organism*	*Person/Agent*
1. What is the nature of the human being?	Mechanistic *Individual* — material and determined — atomized, isolated, and unrelated	Organic *Individual* — living and teleological —aspect of a functional whole	Human *Person* — conscious, free, intentional —person-in-community
2. What is the nature of the social world?	Contractarian *society*	Organic *society*	Personal *community*
3. One or many?	Many (variety)	One (unity)	One and many (unity in variety)
4. What is the basic motive?	Fear	Fear	Love
5. What is the nature of rationality?	Technical-scientific (means-ends pragmatism)	Dialectical (contrast of opposites)	Practical (Aristotle's *phronesis*)
6. What is the nature of social relations?	Competition for power (I-It)	Functional relations of each to all (I-It)	Friendship (I-Thou)
7. Whose interests are sought?	Self-interest (egocentric)	Self-interest (egocentric)	Self and other interest (heterocentric)

Table 4.1 (*cont.*)

Question	*Machine*	*Organism*	*Person/Agent*
8. What is the basic ethical problem?	Achieving cooperation in the face of individuals competing for power	Integrating particular social relations into the whole social system in automatic and functional fashion	Overcoming fear-based hostility by means of loving relationships
9. What is the danger?	Atomism and alienation	Totalitarianism	Ideally none
10. What is the nature of ethics?	Obedience to laws	Good form	Love, friendship, fraternity, community
11. What is the nature of social order?	Order through force	Hierarchical order	Participatory order open to ongoing criticism, challenge, and transformation
12. What are the relevant historical traditions?	— Roman law — Hobbes, Locke — Liberal humanism — Realism	— Greek morality — Plato, Rousseau — Romanticism — Idealism	— Judeo - Christian — Augustine, Aquinas — Communitarianism — Sophisticated realism

Based on Macmurray (1957, 1961)

Caring for and Inquiring about Persons-in-Community

Community integrates the levels of society, as we saw in chapter 2, by means of appreciative caring in the intentional caring relationship. Caring is a "norm for the rightness or wrongness of all action," a norm that enables us "to define morality by reference to maintaining community in action" (Macmurray, 1961, p. 120). This caring and community maintaining norm, moreover, has significant implications for our emerging understanding of reflective-generative practice.

When persons care for each other, according to Macmurray (1961), they behave in the highest ethical fashion and create community. At the core of social relations in general, caring is also the essence of the helping professions — better called the caring professions (Dokecki, 1986). Caring, already explored in detail in chapter 3, is emerging as a central phenomenon in a wide variety of professional intervention contexts (e.g., Hobbs et al., 1984; Imre, 1982; Morris, 1986; Noddings, 1984; Sarason, 1985; Watson, 1980).

As suggested in chapter 3, caring and knowing are inextricably bound up in reflective-generative practice; therefore, professionals must develop a human science methodology adequate to the community of persons in caring relation, adequate to the ethical position developed thus far. What would this human science methodology entail? Let us extend the analysis from earlier chapters.

Knowledge of persons-in-community, on Macmurray's view, may be *impersonal* or *personal*. The traditional sciences impersonally comprehend the deterministic realm of mechanism (as in the physical sciences) and the realm of organism (as in the biological sciences). In the human sciences, however, we can know personally through studies that can deal with meaning, consciousness, freedom, and intentionality, and we can thereby comprehend the ethical realm of the community of persons in caring relation.

The human sciences have their modern root in Kant's critique of the Newtonian claim that natural science can know everything. Accepting Rousseau's assertion that being human entails freedom, Kant argued that natural science causal analysis is inadequate to understanding the person. Traditional natural science causality reduces humans to the determined moving bodies of physics (Bloom, 1987; see also Rychlak, 1981, for an analysis of causality and the person). This claimed inadequacy of the nomothetic natural sciences (*Naturwissenschaften*) to the human realm led to a nineteenth-century call for more idiographic and historical human sciences (*Geisteswissenschaften*).

The positivistic natural science view has been increasingly criticized since the 1950s. We are entering a post-positivist age (see Bernstein, 1976; Brown, 1977; Hanson, 1958/1965; Koch, 1981; Kuhn, 1962/1970; Toulmin, 1953/1960). Contemporary human science, however, is postpositivist, not antiempiricist. In postpositivism, narrow and limited positivist methods are complemented with a variety of methods, chosen to be adequate to particular phenomena in particular contexts.

The postpositivist human sciences reject all methodological claims to be the royal road to knowledge (Bernstein, 1983). This is so since the quest for the Archimedean point of absolutely certain objective knowledge, by positivism or by its methodological competitors, is misguided and has not been achieved. If we cannot achieve absolutely certain objective knowledge in our tragicomic state, however, this doesn't mean we can't achieve any usable knowledge. We can usefully view knowledge as assertoric, as we saw in chapter 2. The assertoric knowledge position suggests that "some knowledge claims are better than others, but none is beyond doubt" (Polkinghorne, 1983, p. 289), and that attaining knowledge entails argumentation and practical reasoning.

Macmurray's viewpoint as it relates to human science methodology suggests that since the person and the community are hierarchically organized at the mechanistic, organic, and personal levels, an adequate methodology requires multiple methods to address these multiple levels. In that regard, Bernstein (1986) has argued that "it is methodologically prudent to be open to different types of research strategy" (p. 74), and Cook (1986) has called for postpositivist critical multiplism.

The fullness of the realm of persons-in-community, then, requires a variety of methods. *The choice of method to address a particular question is an ethical matter, value-laden not automatic* (Dokecki, 1983, 1986, 1990). There have been many nominations of methods for a comprehensive human sciences framework (see Hoshmand, 1989, for a review). Colleagues and I (Dokecki, 1986; Dokecki et al., 1986) proposed a scheme with four components: (1) evaluation research — micro-quantitative; (2) phenomenology — micro-qualitative; (3) behavioral systems analysis — macro-quantitative; and (4) political philosophy — macro-qualitative. Building on this work, Table 4.2 presents a methodological framework for the human sciences. Macmurray's (1957, 1961) philosophy of the community of persons in caring relation integrates its elements.

The structure of the framework suggests that inquiry may be narrow and focused (micro) or broad and inclusive (macro). Inquiry may also be quantitative (impersonal) or qualitative (personal). And, "the impersonal attitude is justifiable when it is itself subordinated to the personal attitude, when it is adopted for the sake of the personal" (Macmurray, 1961, p. 35).

Table 4.2 Human Science Methodological Framework

Scope of Inquiry	Type of Inquiry	
	Quantitative/ Impersonal	*Qualitative/ Personal*
Micro-Level	Experimental and Functional Studies	Interpretive Studies
Macro-Level	Systems-Analytic Studies	Worldview Studies

In *experimental and functional studies* (pertinent to aspects of the mechanistic individual and society), the experiment, cost-effectiveness analysis, and related quantitative methods help us determine the empirical association of variables and cause-effect relationships. This is the traditional realm of most behavioral science research. In *interpretive studies* (pertinent to aspects of the person and community) phenomenological and related qualitative methods yield understanding of personal meanings, intentions, and interpretations of community situations (such as those in which empirical relationships have been found). This has been the realm of many humanistic inquirers. In *systems studies* (pertinent to aspects of the organic individual and society), community, policy, organizational, and related multivariate quantitative methods help us see how focused and delimited cause-effect relationships function in networks or systems of such relationships. This is the realm of many community studies. Finally, in *worldview* (*Weltanschauung*) studies (pertinent to aspects of the person and community), critical, speculative, interpretive, and related qualitative methods, often from the humanities, help us understand whole political and social systems. This form of inquiry helps facilitate decisions among the competing value claims of ideological, political, and ethical worldviews. Modern behavioral science has tended to avoid inquiry in this realm. A human science outlook would see such studies as both legitimate and necessary for a complete understanding of the community.[2]

I do not present this framework as a methodology for all time. It has utility, but more important, it exemplifies what professionals, from the perspective of reflective-generative practice, ought to be about — namely, going

[2] This human science framework is *not* a taxonomy. Its purpose is not to offer a smorgasbord of methodological choices for sampling in "fuzzy headed eclectic" fashion. Rather, as aspects of a conceptually unified (by Macmurray's philosophy) framework, the diflerent methods provide diflerent but complementary perspectives on human development phenomena. In a given research program or professional situation, an inquirer may (a) operate within one quadrant but learn from prior inquiries in other quadrants, (b) perform a set of inquiries using methods from two or more quadrants seriatim, or (c) design any given inquiry by combining methods from two or more quadrants.

beyond positivism by engaging in interventions that address the is-ought discrepancy of the tragicomic human situation from a conceptually integrated, multimethod address to the complex and ethically challenging human phenomena of our world in order to promote human development and community.

The Nature of Community

In this book, I have been developing a framework for professional ethics that, as with jazz, intends mutually to enhance (a) personal freedom and creativity — in short, the human development of clients and professionals, and (b) cooperative action in community. Of particular relevance to this form of professional ethics is the role played by face-to-face communities, which can serve as both the model for and a goal to be achieved in the professional-client relationship. Recall the description in the Introduction of the face-to-face interhuman relations among members of a jazz group. Professionals ought both to create such communities in their relationships with clients and help promote them in their clients' lives. They are the necessary social environments for enhancing human development. Communities are social groupings with common purposes and aims negotiated in face-to-face encounters. They are enduring groups that provide social support and resources for their members. They help enable people to deal with social vulnerability, suffering, and threats to human development (Farley, 1990).

A nurturing and supportive community is essential to meeting the many challenges facing those who choose to enhance human development through caring for others in a sustained and meaningful fashion. Community is a social grouping (e.g., a nurturing family, a nourishing church, a supportive peer group or neighborhood, a compassionate school, a hospice, a reflective-generative professional relationship) that promotes human development. Not just any social grouping is a community in this sense. Indeed, one that hinders human development (e.g., a destructive dysfunctional family, a rigidly dogmatic church or a tyrannical cult, an alienated and hostile neighborhood, a school that menaces, not teaches, children, a sterile nursing home, a sexually exploitive client-professional situation) would be an anti-community. True community, in the context of the tragicomic human situation, enhances human development by increasing mutual aid and shared heritage among people, not demeaning people, not dividing people, and not bestowing unwarranted advantage on people. It strengthens persons and families, enables parents and caregivers to do their jobs well, and respects the rights of individual people of all kinds. Anticommunities are demeaning, divisive, and unfair. They weaken persons and families, parents and other caregivers, and they oppress and thereby present obstacles to human development, even to the point of causing developmental setbacks and regression (Dokecki, 1983; Hobbs et al., 1984; Moroney and Dokecki, 1984).

Human development and community are two sides of the same coin — community promotes human development; persons who develop humanly seek to form or participate in community. Together, they are first principles, fundamental ethical precepts: You ought to promote human development and community because they are fundamental purposes of human existence. In a statement echoing his words opening this chapter, Loewy (1993, pp. 232–33), in his ethics of interdependence, nicely articulated this viewpoint:

> Individuals, necessarily social creatures, cannot (especially in today's world) develop their individual talents and lead their individual lives outside the support the community affords. On the other hand, communities cannot develop and thrive as communities, without developing the unique talents their members possess. A regard for community as well as a respect for the uniqueness of individuals are both essential if one is to support the other so that both may survive. When seen in this way a homeostatic balance between communal and private ends in which ultimately both must be reconciled within the context of common goals and ends seems inevitable. In such a balance community in its own right becomes a value and a goal for the individual and fostering individuality becomes a value and goal for the community.

The correspondence of this passage to the recurring jazz metaphor I have been using is striking. Just as jazz requires creative individuality and both the immediate community of the jazz group and the community embodied in the jazz tradition (Williams, 1959/1993), so does our social life together require concern for *both* person *and* community. The point to be made is that there is a double interdependence: (1) human development promotes community and vice versa, and (2) from the standpoint of ethics, human development and community should be pursued interdependently.

Modern Obstacles to the Quest for Community

As suggested in earlier chapters, modern Western society has problematically come to express agency (masculine) values to the virtual exclusion of communion (feminine) values (Bakan, 1966). Agency (the mechanistic individualistic principle) and communion (the organic community principle) have operated in tension throughout human history, and each person and each society has arrived at its own tragicomic agency-communion blend or balance. The triumph of agency over communion, roughly between the seventeenth and the mid-twentieth centuries, has, however, increasingly come to characterize the modern world. Agentic modernity overthrew the more communal premodern social order: democracy replaced monarchy politically; capitalism replaced feudalism economically; science replaced the church as the guarantor of truth; Protestantism challenged Catholicism; and somewhat more gradually, the egalitarian family has been replacing patriarchy. Although there have been many benefits attendant on agency's triumph over community, particularly concerning increased individual freedom and equality, these gains are beginning to wear thin, and unalloyed agency has become corrosive of the realm of community. The task of our world is *not* to restore the hegemony of communion, since such a pendulum swing back would have many equally corrosive effects in the realm of the person, but to *mitigate agency with communion.*

The quest for community — our tragicomic attempt to mitigate agency with communion — along with loneliness and fear of death are existential facts in the course of our development as fully human persons (Becker, 1968, 1973, 1975; Nisbet, 1953/1990; Sarason, 1985). Society's fundamental ethical task is creating social conditions that enable us to live with these facts in as meaningful, peaceful, and just fashion as possible. In approaching this task, we strive to deal with what is already present in our world that threatens meaning. We do so by nurturing and enhancing what is already there that manifests culture and community. We also try to transcend the "already" in quest for the "not yet." This transcendent dimension of human existence is at the heart of humanity's efforts to generate culture and is very broadly a spiritual endeavor.

The metaphor of *the web* — evocative of generativity, interdependence, and ecology — is useful in giving shape to a public and democratic approach to community. At the personal level, there is the web of life; socially, the moral web. The organization of work and the politics of community building publicly manifest these interrelated webs, ideally serving generativity. Injustice in the productive (work) and reproductive (family) systems, however, erodes the community's generative capacities. We must reorganize work and plan democratically to enhance generativity, and politics should be the exercise of our tragicomic power to that end (Winter, 1989).

Historically, the United States has struggled politically and culturally from the outset with the tension between agency and communion. The spirit of communion has given rise to an important, albeit minority, voice in American culture, expressed by such revered founding figures as Winthrop and Jefferson, and such cultural icons as Melville, Hawthorne, Twain, and more contemporaneously,

Martin Luther King (McWilliams, 1973). The majority voice of individualism was an inevitable outcome of our nation's birth in the escape from European political and religious persecution. Rampant individualism, however, has increasingly become problematic in American society. We sorely need a language of community commitment, reclaiming the best from our early religious and civic traditions, for us even to begin to identify this issue and the possible means of addressing it (Bellah et al., 1985, 1991). Alexis de Toqueville glimpsed some of this situation in his nineteenth-century observation of the importance for the exercise of freedom of the many local groupings and associations that characterized American society. We need to strengthen these intermediate community like structures in the twentieth century, because our fundamental quest for community is often manifest in a tendency toward an over controlling central government in the name of national community. This oppressive societal construction would at best be a pseudocommunity, however, which would seriously detract from, rather than enhance, personal freedom (Nisbet, 1953/1990), what Fromm would call *escape from freedom.* Current draconian legislative proposals to deal with the public's fear about the perceived increase in violent crime should come to mind.

Toward a New Theory of Community: The Third Position

Colleagues and I (Dokecki, 1990, 1992; Dokecki, Newbrough, and O'Gorman, 1992, 1993; Newbrough, 1989, 1992; Newbrough, O'Gorman, Dokecki, and Moroney, 1991; Newbrough, O'Gorman, and Dokecki, 1993; O'Gorman,

Dokecki, and Newbrough, 1993; O'Gorman, Newbrough, and Dokecki, 1995) have been developing a tragicomic *third position* theory of community as an integration of the two classical positions, *Gemeinschaft* (organic and communal emphasis on the one) and *Gesellschaft* (mechanistic and individualistic emphasis on the many), with a dual emphasis on both the one and the many. The third position requires, as with Loewy's ethics of interdependence, a double rather than a single intention: a moral action is one that intends the goal of improving the community as collectivity and, at the same time, the goal of enhancing individual human development, as with the jazz metaphor.

The third community position suggests the importance of communication. John Dewey said that community is conversation, a metaphor for active communication in the community. Combined with Habermas's (1984) theory of communicative competence discussed in chapter 3, community becomes the active process of free and uncoerced conversation. This theory calls for a new tragicomic professional role — to establish and to maintain conversation, in a typically quite pluralistic situation, in pursuit of the public interest and the common good. That role would be filled by, among others, the reflective-generative practitioner, who would be guided by a view of the common good based on the logic used by Jacques Maritain (1947) in *The Person and the Common Good.* On this view, the common good is not utilitarianism's greatest good for the greatest number. Rather, the common good is what is good in common for each and every person — for Maritain (and Aquinas), eternal life with God; for the reflective-generative practitioner, human development and community. Personality theorist Erich Fromm not only used this kind of logic but also espoused a position consistent with reflective-generative practice. For Fromm (1955), in *The Sane Society*, the common good of the human person entails meeting the universal needs (relatedness, transcendence, rootedness, sense of identity, and frame of orientation and devotion) that grow from the human situation. Moreover, Fromm argued that modern society is *insane* because it makes meeting these needs very difficult indeed.

In his last book, *To Have or To Be?*, Fromm (1976) argued that any society that stresses the accumulation of things (*having*) over living lovingly and caringly with other persons (*being*) will fail to enable its members to meet those universal human needs, and thereby it will make a meaningful life impossible to achieve. It is interesting to note that Pope John Paul II used a similar argument in the encyclical *On Social Concern*, where he distinguished between the *under*development characteristic of poverty and the *over* development characteristic of affluence, both of which derive from societal distortions arising in the having orientation (Baum and Ellsberg, 1990).

Third position theory is designed to be a tragicomic critique both of premodernity's organic and of modernity's contractarian political and ethical theories, as with Macmurray. This double critique yields a third position with significant methodological and historical dimensions. The methodological move is toward assertoric rather than apodictic knowledge, toward practical argumentation rather than universal laws (Polkinghorne, 1983). Envisioned is a more developed populace that rationally and actively participates in everyday life — personal, social, economic, and political. The purpose of community life, so conceived, is generativity — the improvement of the local situation (as an interdependent ecology) and the improvement of the people who live there (as humans to be developed). The third position offers a normative ideal of an integrated social ecology that honors liberty, equality, and fraternity — balanced in a dynamic tension to develop a good society (Newbrough, 1992).

The movement toward the ethics of community, argues Newbrough, should be understood in world historical context. Toulmin's (1990) *Cosmopolis: The Hidden Agenda of Modernity* has strongly influenced the work colleagues and I have been doing in developing the theory of the third position. He identified the modern period as beginning in 1648 when the Peace of Westphalia brought the Thirty Years War to a close. It had been a bitter, vicious time of conflict between Catholic organic (communion) interests and Protestant more individualized (agency) interests. It was also a time of social and economic disasters — crop failures, plagues, and the lack of strong political leadership. This war came after the full blooming of the Renaissance in the 1500s, when there was great interest in understanding and supporting humans and their development. The Renaissance humanists, such as Erasmus, Montaigne, and Shakespeare, appreciative of the tragicomic nature of human existence, were urbane, open-minded, and skeptically tolerant. The Peace of Westphalia eschewed much of this humanism in the process of redefining the primary political entity as the nation-state to protect against the power of the Catholic Church. Much of the agenda of modernity, then, has entailed a retreat from tragicomic humanistic values in order to strengthen and advance the political and economic power interests of the nation-states.

In the face of the terrible social conditions that prevailed in Europe during much of the seventeenth century, the tragicomic Renaissance attitude of open-mindedness and tolerance was viewed as allowing, even encouraging, religious conflict to continue. The times called for clear, distinct, and certain ideas. Descartes developed the method of systematic doubt, says Toulmin, as a means for establishing certainty and, thereby, moving to resolve the religious conflict. Through continuous doubting, people could arrive at the foundation of truth. Descartes located that foundation in rational thought and Euclidian geometry as its practical expression. Logic and mathematics became the preferred method in a world that Newton conceived as physical and mechanical. Certainty could be achieved in a confusing and conflict-ridden world through a powerful and agreed upon method. The search for and extension of this method eventually gave rise to science as the prevailing Western mindset, and logical positivism as the dominant philosophy of science.

Logical Positivism, articulated in the early twentieth century by the Vienna Circle and debated throughout much of this century, was devoted to establishing abstract and universal, not *practical*, knowledge. Toulmin describes four intellectual moves that brought it about: (1) from the oral to the written, (2) from the particular to the universal, (3) from the local to the general, and (4) from the timely to the timeless. The driving motivation was a quest for certainty through prediction and control entailing sensory experience and mathematical reasoning, a decidedly anti-transcendent approach. It should be obvious, moreover, that a written, universal, general, and timeless view of knowledge and culture is not particularly conducive to community.

We are, however, no longer true believers in logical positivism. The briefest possible summary of its fate is that the proposition it was trying to prove — transcendent metaphysics is meaningless — came to be seen as a meaningless proposition by its own methodological lights. In addition, intellectuals were disillusioned by the holocaust and the bomb, interpretable as the ultimate outcomes of the scientific attitude, and historically-minded philosophers of science (e.g., Hanson, Toulmin, Kuhn) argued that science was more socially and politically contextual than the searchers for abstract universals could ever defend. Stated in terms of intellectual history, we may say the modern age ended with the collapse of logical positivism, and we are now tragicomically searching for new grounds for rationality and ethics.

The contemporary world, argues Toulmin, is in a situation similar to that of Europe during the Thirty Years War. In this our time, uncertainty and processes of destabilization and change abound. There is a great yearning for community, but we have tended to lose faith in many of the institutions that have traditionally helped provide it, including the family, the church, and the neighborhood. We also yearn for certainty and stability, but we have lost faith in the ability of traditional science to provide them.

Science and philosophy are shifting gears. Rather than speaking of *the scientific method*, there are such notions as *multiple methods* and *triangulation*, as discussed earlier. Proofs are giving way to knowledge claims and assertoric knowledge (Polkinghorne, 1983). In the social and behavioral sciences, qualitative methods and the use of narrative are becoming acceptable, under the rubric of human science. We are rediscovering practical knowledge (Aristotle's *phronesis*), with a resurgence of interest in the Pragmatism of Charles Sanders Peirce, William James, and John Dewey (Bernstein, 1971, 1976, 1983, 1992; Dokecki, 1987). The quest for community — the tragicomic mitigation of agency with communion — then, is taking place at a time of more openness in science to multiple methods and sources of knowing (Dokecki, 1992). There are parallels, of course, between the call for tolerance and open-mindedness in method and the call for these charitable attitudes in our life together in community.

Toulmin (1982) takes a tragicomic and constructive position. While many today are methodologically deconstructive, arguing that we must live and pursue our intellectual pursuits without any overarching stories (Lyotard, 1984), Toulmin argues from a methodologically constructive position that this anticosmological viewpoint grew from our initial love affair and subsequent disillusionment with scientific rationality. He asserts that it is unreasonable to dismiss the possibility of a coherent and comprehensive outlook that shows how all the pieces fit into the whole and where we fit in the grand scheme of things. We need to search tentatively for an overarching story, a root metaphor (Pepper, 1942) — a *cosmology* — that is intellectually defensible and that holds the promise of meeting what Fromm identifies as the basic human need for a frame of orientation. Toulmin's nomination for this return to cosmology is *ecology*. Ecology entails the argument, from a living systems standpoint, that living creatures must be understood in the context of the total environment, which itself is structured in interdependent fashion. In this regard, recall Erikson's theory of generativity as the "Ethics of Human Ecology" (Browning, 1973, p. 151) and Dewey and Bentley's (1949) transactionalism, which views human action as an interdependent function of person-in-environment.

Thus far, my exposition of third position theory has mostly dealt with community as environment. The mention in this chapter of personality theorists Fromm and Erikson, however, suggests two important person-level psychological dimensions of a meaningful theory of community. These are (1) the degree to which we experience our social world as community, the *psychological sense of community* (McMillan and Chavis, 1986; Sarason, 1974), and (2) the degree to which we experience ourselves as competent and effective community members, our beliefs of *self-efficacy* (Bandura, 1989). Members of communities as viewed through the lens of third position theory would not only be expected to grow "objectively" as persons, but also to report the experience of being connected, supported, and cared for in their social relationships. And intertwined with this psychological sense of community is the belief that we are powerful and self-efficacious, that is, in control of our lives and capable of intentionally affecting others.

On the view of third position theory, self-efficacious and tragicomic persons with a sense of community are those who live within true communities, develop humanly, and construct and enact a generative narrative. As mentioned earlier, one way of viewing the ethical imperative for reflective-generative practice is to say that it ought to help clients create or develop a meaningful generative narrative, which would contribute to professionals' tragicomic generative narrative as well. This is the rationale for the project I assign my ethics students described in chapter 3.

Third position theory, then, argues for the interpenetration of the themes of community, human development, psychological sense of community, personal belief in self-efficacy, the personal narrative, and ethics. All these would ideally be enacted through the promotion of the caring and competent community. What does this mean?

The Ethics of Reflective-Generative Practice and the Caring and Competent Community[3]

The social ideal, tragicomically pursued, of the caring and competent community is a slight variation on the theme of the competent and caring society, which I developed along with colleagues in a family-oriented social policy project that resulted in the publication of *Strengthening Families* (Hobbs et al., 1984). Much of our analysis was counter to the American policy-analytic tradition with its emphasis on economics-based cost-effectiveness and cost-benefit analyses and their claimed value neutrality. We operated more out of the British school of policy analysis represented in Richard Titmuss's value-oriented analysis, especially in his *The Gift Relationship*. In that book, Titmuss (1971) analyzed the systems that provided blood for medical purposes in the United States and Great Britain using a combination of methods influenced by value considerations. In effect, he compared two value systems: America's, with its market-oriented use of blood selling and of donating earmarked

[3] Material in this section was originally presented in somewhat altered form in Dokecki (1983) and Hobbs et al. (1984).

for particular persons, and Britain's, with its prohibition of selling and earmarking and its requirement that blood be donated voluntarily and freely to unknown others, strangers, for the common welfare of all. He found that blood was both more readily available and freer of disease and other imperfections under the British system. In the Titmuss tradition, social policy and social policy analysis are matters of values and ethics beyond technology and economics.

The notion of the caring and competent community grows from this form of value-oriented analysis. Not that there weren't empirical aspects of the Titmuss and the Hobbs et al. analyses. For example, we extensively studied child care and parent education and their relationship to community environments and public policy, both historically and contemporaneously. We also looked closely at the evidence on psychological sense of community and found that, "in communities, individuals experience a sense of membership, influence members of the group and are themselves in turn influenced by others, have personal needs fulfilled, and share a psychologically and personally satisfying connection with others" (findings reported by McMillan, 1976, as quoted in Hobbs et al., p. 41). We combined traditional policy analysis with a value analysis based on the ethics of human development and community. Here I present some of the results of that analysis, which had a policy focus, modifying it to fit with many ideas that have emerged since the publication of *Strengthening Families* in 1984 and influenced the development of the ethics of the tragicomic reflective-generative practice.

The professional intervention ethical framework for

reflective-generative practice, tragicomically conceived, reflects a preference for a developmental and social ecological perspective and its attendant value positions (Bronfenbrenner, 1977; Emery and Trist, 1972; Hobbs, 1975). I intend it to be useful for, among many purposes: the formation of social intervention questions to be asked of the existing knowledge base on professional practice and research; the organization of existing data, information, and opinions; the analysis of the existing practice and policy context; the presentation of arguments for and against proposed practice and policy options; and the formulation of practice and policy evaluation strategies. The framework is grounded in the view, as with Macmurray, that the family is our key human development system and that this community like system is as necessary for community as community is for it.

The framework's basic value position is that *the central goal of professional intervention is to enhance human development through community*. This value position can be stated in two forms:

1. The aim of professional intervention should be to *enhance community* (both the local, face-to face community and the broader national community) so that individuals and their families have a legitimate claim on community resources and support in the performance of their developmental tasks.
2. The aim of professional intervention should be to *enhance human development* so that individuals and their families can participate effectively in the community. The community can legitimately expect individuals and families to master their developmental tasks and engage

in relationships of reciprocal responsibility with the community.

This basic value requires elaboration through posing several specific *value-based questions* with their associated *criteria.* The result is an illustration of the form community ethics for reflective-generative practice might take, especially in the realms of public policy and program development and evaluation.

Value Element 1: Does the Professional Intervention Enhance Community?

Professional practices that promote the coming together of people around shared values and the pursuit of common cause enhance community at both the local, face-to-face level, and the national level, where people also concern themselves with the well-being of persons who are strangers to them.

The *first criterion* is, Does the professional intervention increase shared heritage, mutual aid, and community building? This criterion launches reflective-generative professionals immediately into the realm of beneficence beyond nonmaleficence. Interventions are valued that actively bring persons together both locally (diversity of communities) and nationally (overarching communities, encompassing diverse local communities). These professional interventions highlight human commonalities and aspects of shared heritage, thereby encouraging people to form socially around shared values and common goals. They encourage placing human differences in appropriate perspective, recognizing that the uniqueness of individuals is not a cause for suspicion and separation but is, rather, socially valuable. These forms of intervention help raise consciousness about matters of far-reaching societal concern. They are implemented fairly and even-handedly so that all persons feel equitably treated. Developing *commons* — community areas and functions shared by all, such as libraries, public schools, and the like — and setting up representative participative bodies to govern these community functions are among the means to achieve these purposes. These professional interventions also encourage the formation of self-help groups, caring opportunities, and community organizations that work to better their members as well as promote community well-being.

The *second criterion* is, Is the professional intervention demeaning to any group? Professional practices are opposed when they demean people by their nature or by specific forms of implementation. Demeaning practices subject persons to humiliating circumstances and communicate that those who participate have an inferior status. Such practices are most often implemented through means-tested eligibility determination, a process by which eligibility for a program or service is assessed on the basis of a combination of factors, including income, assets, and family size. Any conspicuous setting apart of groups of people (as in some health-screening programs) also communicates the status of inferiority. Participants are thereby devalued and stigmatized, often suffering a loss of self-esteem. Many persons are loathe to seek the supposed benefits offered by such practices and may thereby suffer harm. Demeaning professional interventions are unjust and deny the existence of common needs among people and clearly reinforce the idea that not all persons are equal.

The *third criterion* is, Does the professional intervention bestow unwarranted advantage? Practices that give unwarranted advantage are opposed. Comparative justice requires that like cases be treated alike and different cases be treated differently. Certain differences — those based on the notion that special needs, justified as societally importance, call for special help — may result in advantages that are warranted. In this case, all members of a justifiable special-need group should have entitlement to the intervention's warranted advantage. Where advantages are bestowed that do not respond to justifiable societal need, however, they are unwarranted (Watson, 1980).

The *fourth criterion* is, Is the professional intervention divisive? Practices that are socially divisive are opposed because, by definition, they work against social coherence and solidarity, which are required for meaningful community. Divisive professional interventions separate persons for unwarranted reasons on the basis of age, sex, racial and ethnic group membership, socioeconomic status, religious preference, sexual orientation, educational level, handicapping condition, and the like. These practices create situations that allow, even encourage, invidious social comparisons, which tend to divide people who might otherwise engage in fruitful social relationships. Certain professional interventions that divide people may be warranted if they allow receipt of warranted advantages (as defined in the previous criterion). Although a core of shared values is necessary for fostering a sense of community and a sense of group identity, impermeable boundaries that arbitrarily define people in and out of social groupings are destructive of community.

The concern in this criterion is with numerous policies

and practices that divide major groups. These include de jure and de facto segregation; the separation of old people in nursing homes; and the continuing inequities between men and women at work. Further examples include those human services that are delivered in decidedly different ways for rich and poor people or that use separate modes of payment (for example, Blue Cross versus Medicaid), often leading to differential quality of service.

Value Element 2: Does the Professional Intervention Strengthen Families?

Strong families are the foundation of meaningful community, and they provide the context for the human development of their members. In addition, the family as a system has developmental tasks to master and has responsibilities for relating to other systems within society.

The *first criterion* is, Does the professional intervention improve the capacity of families to master a broad range of developmental tasks? Practices are valued that create conditions enhancing parental competence, especially in relation to intrafamily and extrafamily factors that influence childrearing. Such practices improve the knowledge, skill, and decision-making capacity of parents in dealing with family developmental issues, such as pregnancy and childbirth, children's growth and developmental tasks, children's health and nutrition, family needs for child care provision because of parental work responsibilities, and children's entry into school. These professional interventions provide for assessing the diverse needs of individual families, recognizing that different families face different developmental tasks and that the same family has different developmental needs at different times in its life cycle. Of importance here are reflective-generative professional interventions that enhance family functioning both in and outside the home.

The *second criterion* is, Does the professional intervention improve the liaison or linkage functions of families as they relate to the social resources and supports they need? Practices are valued when they recognize that families exist within a network of informal social support and formal human service agencies and when they help parents identify and make use of these networks as necessary. Valued professional interventions help parents look toward primary kinds of social support, such as family members, kinship groups, neighbors, and voluntary associations. Formal services should provide information, referral, and liaison services. The goal of such reflective-generative professional interventions is to identify family needs, locate the informal and formal resources necessary for meeting those needs, and help link families with the identified resources. Of concern here are practices that inform families of available resources and facilitate access to those resources.

The *third criterion* is, Does the professional intervention protect the family from unwarranted intrusion and allow parents choice? Policies of voluntary participation in human service programs and practices that intrude as little as possible into private family matters are valued. Short of the danger of physical harm to a family member, participation should not be coercive. Both de jure coercion and the use of blatant or subtle social pressure should be avoided. Beyond these initial criteria of intrusion and choice, practices that provide a variety of options, as well as adequate information about options, are valued insofar as they allow parents to have real choices on decisions they will make regarding their families.

Value Element 3: Does the Professional Intervention Enable Parents To Do Their Job Well?

Enabling parents is the primary means for strengthening families. Reflective-generative practices that enable parents to make competent decisions for their family strengthen the family and enhance the well-being, developmental status, and rights of all family members.

The *first criterion* is, Does the professional intervention minimize stress by making essential resources available to parents? Practices are valued when they help ensure that parents have the time, energy, knowledge, and resources (and consequent satisfaction in the form of positive affect and feelings of worth) necessary to carry out their parental functions well.

The *second criterion* is, Does the professional intervention promote partnership and shared responsibility among parents and service providers, including professionals? Reflective-generative practices that operate according to enablement and empowerment principles are valued. Parents become able to develop and to become effective decision-makers when they are treated as capable adults and are helped by service organizations and professionals to become even more capable. Enablement involves the enhancement of knowledge and skill through appropriate education for adults. Empowerment involves providing parents with resources and legal rights so that they may negotiate effectively with social institutions. Many professionals, primarily because of their training, often behave as imperious Model I experts (chapter 3), an approach decidedly counter to this criterion.

Value Element 4: Does the Professional Intervention Enhance Individual Development and Protect the Rights of Individual Members of the Family?

All family members have ongoing developmental tasks to master. Similarly, all family members, including even very young children, have fundamental human rights.

The *first criterion* is, Does the intervention enhance individual opportunities for the development of competence, self-realization, and self-efficacy? Reflective-generative practices that create conditions or provide services to enhance individuals' physical, cognitive, affective, and interpersonal development are valued. Such practices emphasize that the developmental and educational opportunities of specific family members should not be ignored in the general quest to strengthen the family. This is central to the idea of building a caring and competent community, for it is important to each person that there be developed in the community a diversity of competencies essential to its economic and humane development and that there be a minimum level of competence in basic and special skills above which all persons will be sustained.

The *second criterion* is, Does the professional intervention protect individual members of the family from abuse and severe neglect? Practices are valued that recognize the importance of parental rights to the maintenance of the family unit but that stop short of allowing these rights to work to the significant detriment of individual family members. Issues of child abuse and spouse abuse are involved here. One of the intended effects of many human service programs is to help prevent abuse and severe neglect. Fundamental to this criterion is the concept of the dignity of each human being, but also stressed is the idea that individuals exist in social context and that individual rights, inside or outside the family, imply corresponding social responsibilities.

These, then, are among the values and criteria for the ethics of reflective-generative practice in pursuit of the caring and competent community. They give further specification to the prima facie duties of respect for the autonomy of persons, nonmaleficence, beneficence, and justice identified earlier as the hallmarks of ethical professional practice. In many ethical systems, particularly in the tradition of modern liberalism and libertarianism, nonmaleficence is recognized, but there is great reluctance to go beyond this ethical minimum because of the fear that individual rights may thereby be violated, in effect, doing of harm (Gaylin, 1978). An ethical system intending to promote the caring and competent community, however, must push beyond the ethical minimum. "The obligation individuals have toward each other and to their community and the obligation communities have toward their members," argued Loewy (1993, p. 231), "are beyond the merely minimal ones of mutual non-harm. Unless beneficent obligations are accepted and acted upon, collectives will have little cohesion. They will lack solidarity." Moreover, "if the obligation to strive for the survival of our species (and, for that matter, so that the species can survive to strive for the survival of the ecosystem) is acknowledged as an obligation we all have," he continued, "then obligations . . . must inevitably include obligations of beneficence and caring" (p. 231). Reflective-generative practice, then, requires an ethical outlook that transcends the individual and moves to the level of persons-in-community. The resulting ethics intends to promote the caring and competent community.

Conclusion

I am writing this book during an age in which Gorbachev went to the Vatican to court the pope, whereas fifty years earlier Stalin arrogantly asked how many divisions the pope had — Toulmin (1990) would call this a shift to *moral influence* from coercive and manipulative power as the force that creates and legitimizes social change. Another apparent shift, this time in American cultural values, is from the self-preoccupation of the 1980s to a concern for the public purpose as we move toward the twenty-first century (Schlesinger, 1986). In a related vein, Robert Bellah and his colleagues (1985, 1991) challenge us to develop new, more communal habits of the heart as we attempt to reform our individualism-dominated public institutions in pursuit of the good society. And we have the appearance of *The Responsive Community* — a new journal of American communitarianism that brings together people from across a surprisingly wide political spectrum — which calls for a balancing of rights and responsibilities.

Yet this is also a time of national and international ethnic, racial, and religious conflict — Senator Daniel Patrick Moynihan (1993) has called this state of affairs *pandemonium,* Milton's term for hell in *Paradise Lost.* Clearly, we are struggling to mitigate agency with communion in our tragicomic world. This tumultuous condition is influencing professionals just as they are participating in the formation of a new ethics and social vision. I am calling here for professionals, in the spirit of the jazz metaphor, to practice the ethics of reflective-generative practice in pursuit of the common good of human development and community. They would thereby be joining other like-minded persons in the tragicomic task of rolling a very large ethical rock up a very steep societal hill. But no less is called for in undertaking the project of working toward the caring and competent community.

Bibliography

Abramowitz, C. V., and Dokecki, P. R. (1977). The politics of clinical judgment: Early empirical returns. *Psychological Bulletin, 84,* 460–76.

Bakan, D. (1966). *The duality of human existence: An essay on psychology and religion.* Chicago: Rand McNally.

Bandura, A. (1989). Human agency in social cognitive theory. *American Psychologist, 44,* 1175–84.

Baum, G., and Ellsberg, R. (1990). *The logic of solidarity: Commentaries on Pope John Paul II's encyclical On Social Concern.* Maryknoll, NY: Orbis Books.

Beauchamp, T. L., and Childress, J. F. (1994). *Principles of biomedical ethics* (4th ed.). New York: Oxford University Press.

Becker, E. (1968). *The structure of evil: An essay on the unification of the science of man.* New York: Braziler.

——— (1973). *The denial of death.* New York: Free Press.

——— (1975). *Escape from evil.* New York: Free Press.

Bellah, R. N., Madsen, R., Sullivan, W. M., Swidler, A., and Tipton, S. M. (1985). *Habits of the heart: Individualism and commitment in American life.* New York: Harper and Row.

Bellah, R. N., Madsen, R., Sullivan, W. M., Swidler, A., and Tipton, S. M. (1991). *The good society.* New York: Knopf.

Berger, P. L., and Luckmann, T. (1966). *The social construction of reality.* New York: Doubleday.

Bernstein, R. J. (1971). *Praxis and action: Contemporary philosophies of human activity*. Philadelphia: University of Pennsylvania Press.

——— (1976). *The restructuring of social and political theory*. Philadelphia: University of Pennsylvania Press.

——— (1983). *Beyond objectivism and relativism: Science, hermeneutics, and praxis*. Philadelphia: University of Pennsylvania Press.

——— (1986). *Philosophical profiles: Essays in a pragmatic mode*. Philadelphia: University of Pennsylvania Press.

——— (1992). *The new constellation: The ethical-political horizons of modernity/postmodernity*. Cambridge, MA: MIT Press.

Bloom, A. (1987). *The closing of the American mind*. New York: Simon and Schuster.

Bok, S. (1978). *Lying: Moral choice in public and private life*. New York: Pantheon.

Bronfenbrenner, U. (1977). Toward an experimental ecology of human development. *American Psychologist, 32*, 513–31.

Brown, H. I., (1977). *Perception, theory and commitment: The new philosophy of science*. Chicago: University of Chicago Press.

Browning, D. S. (1973). *Generative man: Psychoanalytic perspectives*. Philadelphia: Westminster Press.

——— (1991). *A fundamental practical theology*. Minneapolis, MN: Fortress Press.

Bruner, J. (1990). *Acts of meaning*. Cambridge, MA: Harvard University Press.

Buber, M. (1958). *I and Thou* (2nd ed.). New York: Scribners.

Callahan, D. (1984). Autonomy: A moral good, not a moral obsession. *Hastings Center Report, 14* (5), 40–42.

Cook, T. D. (1986). Postpositivist critical multiplism. In L. Schotland and M. M. Mark (eds.). *Social science and social policy* (pp. 21–62). Beverly Hills, CA: Sage.

Craig, J. H., and Craig, M. (1973). *Synergic power: Beyond domination and submissiveness*. Berkeley, CA: Proactive Press.

Dewey, J., and Bentley, A. (1949). *Knowing and the known*. Boston: Beacon Press.

Dokecki, P. R. (1983). The place of values in the world of psychology and public policy. *Peabody Journal of Education, 60* (3), 108–25.

——— (1986). Methodological futures of the caring professions. *Urban and Social Change Review, 19* (Winter, Summer), 3–7.

——— (1987). Can knowledge contribute to the creation of community? *Journal of Community Psychology, 15,* 90–96.

——— (1990). On knowing the person as agent in caring relation. *Person-Centered Review, 5,* 155–69.

——— (1992). On knowing the community of caring persons: A methodological basis for the reflective-generative practice of community psychology. *Journal of Community Psychology, 20,* 26–35.

Dokecki, P. R., Able, H., Allred, K., Beck, B., Donovan, Jr., W., Heflinger, C. A., Lowitzer, A., and Smith, S. (1986). Scholars and ethics: Toward an ethically relevant agenda for scholarly inquiry in mental retardation. In P. R. Dokecki and R. M. Zaner (eds.), *Ethics in dealing with persons with severe handicaps: Toward a research agenda* (pp. 17–37). Baltimore: Paul H. Brookes.

Dokecki, P. R., Newbrough, J. R., and O'Gorman, R. T. (1992, August). *In pursuit of a new theory of community: Community psychology and contextual theology in conversation.* A roundtable presented at the annual meetings of the American Psychological Association, Washington, D.C.

Dokecki, P. R., Newbrough, J. R., and O'Gorman, R. T. (1993). Community and leadership in the postmodern church: III. Leadership for Community. *PACE, 23* (December), 36–40.

Dokecki, P. R., and Zaner, R. M. (Eds.). (1986). *Ethics of dealing with persons with severe handicaps: Toward a research agenda.* Baltimore: Paul H. Brookes.

Dunst, C. J., Trivette, C. M., and Deal, A. G. (1988). *Enabling and empowering families.* Cambridge, MA: Brookline Books.

Emery, F. E., and Trist, E. L. (1972). *Toward a social ecology: Contextual appreciations of the future in the present.* London: Plenum.

Erikson, E. H. (1967). *Insight and responsibility.* New York: Norton.

Farley, E. (1990). *Good & Evil: Interpreting a human condition.* Minneapolis, MN: Fortress Press.

Fischer, F. (1980). *Politics, values, and public policy: The problem of methodology.* Boulder: Westview Press.

Fletcher, J. (1966). *Situation ethics: The new morality.* Philadelphia: Westminster Press.

Forrester, J. (1983). Critical theory and organizational analysis. In G. Morgan (ed.), *Beyond method: Strategies for social research* (pp. 234–46). Beverly Hills, CA: Sage.

Frankena, W. K. (1963/1973). *Ethics.* Englewood Cliffs, NJ: Prentice-Hall.

Fromm, E. (1955). *The sane society.* New York: Rinehart.

——— (1976). *To have or to be?* New York: Bantam.

Gaylin, W. (1978). *Doing good: The limits of benevolence.* New York: Pantheon.

Gergen, K. J. (1978). Toward generative theory. *Journal of Personality and Social Psychology, 36,* 1344–1360.

Geuss, R. (1981). *The idea of a critical theory: Habermas and the Frankfurt School.* New York: Cambridge University Press.

Habermas, J. (1984). *The theory of communicative action.* Boston: Beacon Press.

Hanson, N. R. (1958/1965). *Patterns of discovery.* Cambridge: Cambridge University Press.

Hobbs, N. (1966). Helping disturbed children: Psychological and ecological strategies. *American Psychologist, 21,* 1105–15.

——— (1975). *The futures of children.* San Francisco: Jossey-Bass.

——— (1982). *The troubled and troubling child: Re-Education in mental health, education, and human services programs for children and youth.* San Francisco: Jossey-Bass.

Hobbs, N., Dokecki, P. R., Hoover-Dempsey, K. V., Moroney, R. M., Shayne, M. W., and Weeks, K. H. (1984). *Strengthening families.* San Francisco: Jossey-Bass.

Hoshmand, L. T. (1989). Alternate research paradigms: A

review and teaching proposal. *The Counseling Psychologist, 17*, 3–79.

Imre, R. W. (1982). *Knowing and caring.* New York: University Press of America.

Kaplan, A. (1964). *The conduct of inquiry: Methodology for behavioral science.* San Francisco: Chandler.

Keith-Spiegel, P. and Koocher, G. P. (1985). *Ethics in psychology.* New York: Random House.

Kelly, G. A. (1955). *The psychology of personal constructs.* New York: Norton.

Kirkpatrick, F. G. (1986). *Community: A trinity of models.* Washington, DC: Georgetown University Press.

Koch, S. (1981). The nature and limits of psychological knowledge: Lessons of a century qua "science." *American Psychologist, 36*, 257–69.

Kuhn, T. S. (1962/1970). *The structure of scientific revolutions:* (2nd ed.). Chicago: University of Chicago Press.

Lebacqz, K. (1985). *Professional ethics: Power and paradox.* Nashville, TN: Abingdon Press.

Levinas, E. (1961/1969). *Totality and infinity.* Pittsburgh, PA: Duquesne University Press.

Loewy, E. H. (1993). *Freedom and community: The ethics of interdependence.* Albany: State University of New York Press.

Lyotard, J. F. (1984). *The postmodern condition.* Minneapolis, MN: University of Minnesota Press.

MacIntyre, A. (1966). *A short history of ethics.* New York: Macmillan.

——— (1981). *After virtue.* Notre Dame, IN: University of Notre Dame Press.

Macmurray, J. (1957). *The self as agent.* London: Faber, Ltd.

——— (1961). *Persons in relation.* New York: Harper and Bros.

Maritain, J. (1947). *The person and the common good.* New York: Scribners.

Marrow, A. (1969). *The practical theorist: The life and work of Kurt Lewin.* New York: Basic Books.

Mayeroff, M. (1971). *On caring.* New York: Harper and Row.

McMillan, D. (1976). *Sense of community.* Nashville, TN: George Peabody College.

McMillan, D. W., and Chavis, D. M. (1986). Sense of community: A definition and theory. *Journal of Personality and Social Psychology, 14,* 6–23.

McWilliams, W. C. (1973). *The idea of fraternity in America.* Berkeley: University of California Press.

Moroney, R. M. (1986). *Shared responsibility: Families and social policy.* New York, NY: Aldine.

Moroney, R. M., and Dokecki, P. R. (1984). The family and the professions: Implications for public policy. *Journal of Family Issues, 5,* 224–38.

Morris, R. (1986). *Rethinking social welfare: Why care for the stranger?* New York: Longman.

Moynihan, D. P. (1993). *Pandemonium: Ethnicity in international politics.* New York: Oxford University Press.

Newbrough, J. R. (1989, June). *Toward a theory of community for community psychology.* Invited address presented to the 22nd Interamerican Congress of Psychology, Buenos Aires, Argentina.

——— (1992). Community psychology in the post-modern world. *Journal of Community Psychology, 20,* 10–25.

Newbrough, J. R., O'Gorman, R. T., Dokecki, P. R., and Moroney, R. M. (1991, June). *Toward a postmodern approach to community research and action.* Symposium presented at the Third Biennial Conference on Community Research and Action, Tempe, Arizona.

Newbrough, J. R., O'Gorman, R. T., and Dokecki, P. R. (1993). Community and leadership in the postmodern church: II. The St. Robert Consultation Project. *PACE, 23* (November), 31–35.

Nietzsche, F. (1872/1993). *The birth of tragedy.* London: Penguin Books.

Nisbet, R. A. (1953/1990). *The quest for community: A study in the ethics of order and freedom.* San Francisco: ICS Press.

Noddings, N. (1984). *Caring: A feminine approach to ethics and moral education.* Berkeley: University of California Press.

O'Gorman, R. T., Dokecki, P. R., and Newbrough, J. R. (1993). Community and leadership in the postmodern church: I. Lessons from Latin America — the Basic Ecclesial Communities. *PACE, 23* (October), 29–33.

O'Gorman, R. T., Newbrough, J. R., and Dokecki, P. R. (1995, June). *Communiogenesis: A conversation between theology and community psychology.* Symposium presented at the Fifth Biennial Conference on Community Research and Action, Chicago, IL.

Pepper, S. (1942). *World hypotheses.* Berkeley, CA: University of California Press.

Polkinghorne, D. E. (1983). *Methodology for the human science: Systems of inquiry.* Albany: State University of New York Press.

——— (1988). *Narrative knowing and the human sciences.* Albany: State University of New York Press.

Pope, K. S., Sonne, J. L., and Holroyd, J. (1993). *Sexual feelings in psychotherapy.* Washington, DC: American Psychological Association.

Rawls, J. A. (1971). *Theory of justice.* Cambridge, MA: Harvard University Press.

Rhodes, W. C. (1972). *Behavioral threat and community response: A community psychology inquiry.* New York: Behavioral Publications.

——— (1978). *Emotionally disturbed and deviant children.* Englewood Cliffs, NJ: Prentice Hall.

Ricoeur, P. (1970). *Freud and philosophy: An essay in interpretation* (translated by D. Savage). New Haven, CT: Yale University Press.

Riger, S. (1993). What's wrong with empowerment. *American Journal of Community Psychology, 21,* 279–92.

Rychlak, J. F. (1981). *Introduction to personality and psychotherapy: A theory-construction approach* (2nd ed.). Boston: Houghton Miffin.

Sarason, S. B. (1974). *The psychological sense of community.* San Francisco: JosseyBass.

——— (1985). *Caring and compassion in clinical practice.* San Francisco: Jossey-Bass.

Schlesinger, A. (1986). *The cycles of American history.* Boston: Houghton Mifflin.

Schneiders, S. M. (1989). Spirituality in the academy. *Theological Studies, 50,* 676–97.

Schön, D. (1983). *The reflective practitioner.* New York: Basic Books.

——— (1987). *Educating the reflective practitioner.* San Francisco: Jossey-Bass.

Schutz, A. (1967). *The phenomenology of the social world.* Evanston, IL: Northwestern University Press.

Sokoly, M. M., and Dokecki, P. R. (1992). Ethical perspectives on family-centered early intervention. *Infants and Young Children, 4* (4), 23–32.

Sonne, J. L., and Pope, K. S. (1993). Treating victims of therapist-patient sexual involvement. In K. S. Pope, J. L. Sonne, and J. Holroyd, *Sexual feelings in psychotherapy* (pp. 237–67). Washington, DC: American Psychological Association.

Stout, J. (1988). *Ethics after Babel: The languages of morals and their discontents.* Boston: Beacon Press.

Tillich, P. (1952). *The courage to be.* New Haven: Yale University Press.

Titmuss, R. M. (1971). *The gift relationship: From blood to social policy.* New York: Pantheon.

Toulmin, S. (1950/1986). *The place of reason in ethics.* Chicago: University of Chicago Press.

——— (1953). *The philosophy of science: An introduction.* New York: Harper and Row.

——— (1982). *The return to cosmology: Postmodern science and the theology of nature.* Berkeley: University of California Press.

——— (1990). *Cosmopolis: The hidden agenda of modernity.* New York: Free Press.

Tracy, D. (1987). *Plurality and ambiguity: Hermeneutics, religion, hope.* San Francisco: Harper and Row.

Veatch, R. M. (1984). Autonomy's temporary triumph. *Hastings Center Report, 14* (5), 39–40.

——— (1986). *The foundations of justice: Why the retarded and the rest of us have claims to equality.* New York: Oxford University Press.

Waterman, A. S. (1981). Individualism and interdependence. *American Psychologist, 36,* 762–73.

Watson, D. (1980). *Caring for strangers.* London: Routledge and Kegan Paul.

White, S. W. (1991). *Privileged information.* New York: Viking.

Williams, M. T. (1959/1993). *The jazz tradition.* New York: Oxford University Press.

Winter, G. (1966). *Elements for a social ethic.* New York: Macmillan.

——— (1989). *Community and spiritual transformation.* New York: Crossroad.

Zaner, R. M. (1988). *Ethics and the clinical encounter.* Englewood Cliffs, NJ: Prentice Hall.

Index